JOY Builders

13 Fun Filled Bible Lessons About Joy

Susan L. Lingo

STANDARD PUBLISHING

Cincinnati, Ohio

DEDICATION

You have made known to me the path of life;
you will fill me with joy in your presence.
Psalm 16:11

Joy Builders
© 2001 Susan L. Lingo

Published by Standard Publishing, Cincinnati, Ohio
A division of Standex International Corporation

Credits

Produced by Susan L. Lingo, Bright Ideas Books™
Cover design by Diana Walters
Illustrated by Marilynn G. Barr and Megan E. Jeffery

08 07 06 05 04 03 02 01 5 4 3 2 1
ISBN 0-7847-1234-4
Printed in the United States of America

CONTENTS

INTRODUCTION

POWERING UP YOUR KIDS' FAITH!

Congratulations! You are about to embark on a wonderful and powerful mission to strengthen, energize, and stabilize your kids' faith and fundamental knowledge of God—faith and fundamentals that will launch your kids powerfully into the twenty-first century!

Joy Builders is part of the Power Builders Series, an exciting and powerfully effective curriculum that includes *Faith Finders, Servant Leaders, Disciple Makers, Value Seekers, Peace Makers, Hope Finders, Power Boosters,* and the book you're now holding. *Joy Builders* is dedicated to exploring where joy comes from and how Jesus brings us joy today and promises us joy for all our tomorrows. Thirteen theme-oriented lessons will help your kids explore, assess, and apply God's truths that relate to discovering joy and experiencing the joy of Jesus in both good times and bad. And woven throughout each lesson is Scripture, Scripture, and more Scripture!

Each lesson in *Joy Builders* has the following features:

POWER FOCUS (Approximate time: 10 minutes)—You'll begin with a mighty motivator to get kids thinking about the focus of the lesson. This may include an eye-popping devotion, a simple game, or another lively attention-getting tool. Also included are interactive discussion and a brief overview of what kids will be learning during the lesson. *Purpose: To focus attention and cue kids in to what they'll be learning during the lesson.*

MIGHTY MESSAGE (Approximate time: 15 minutes)—This is the body of the lesson and includes engaging Bible passages that actively teach about the lesson's theme. The Mighty Message is not just "another Bible story," so your kids will discover God's truths through powerful passages and important portions of Scripture that are supported by additional verses and made relevant to kids' lives. Processing questions help kids explore each side of the passages and their relation to the theme, beginning with easier questions for young children and ending with more challenging think-about-it questions for older kids. Meaty and memorable, this lesson section will help kids learn tremendous truths! *Purpose: To teach powerful biblical truths and offer thought-provoking discussion in age-appropriate ways.*

MESSAGE IN MOTION (Approximate time: 10-15 minutes)—This section contains engaging activities that enrich and reinforce the lesson theme. It may include creative crafts, lively games and relays, action songs and rhythmic raps, mini service projects, and much more. *Purpose: To enrich learning in memorable and fun ways that build a sense of community.*

SUPER SCRIPTURE (Approximate time: 10-15 minutes)—This all-important section encourages and helps kids effectively learn, understand, and apply God's Word in their lives. The Mighty Memory Verse was chosen so every child can effectively learn it during the course of three weeks, but an extra-challenge verse is offered for older kids or children who can handle learning more verses. You are free to substitute your own choice of verses in this section, but please keep in mind that the activities, songs, crafts, and mnemonic devices are designed for the Mighty Memory Verse and the accompanying extra-challenge verse. And remember, when it comes to learning God's Word, effective learning takes place when kids work on only one or two verses over the course of several weeks! *Purpose: To memorize, learn, recall, and use God's Word.*

POWERFUL PROMISE (Approximate time: 5-10 minutes)—The lesson closes with a summary, a promise, and a prayer. You'll summarize the lesson, the Mighty Memory Verse, and the theme, then challenge kids to make a special commitment to God for the coming week. The commitments are theme-related and give kids a chance to put their faith into action. Finally, a brief prayer and responsive farewell blessing end the lesson. *Purpose: To make a commitment of faith to God and express thanks and praise to him.*

POWER PAGE! (Take-home paper)—Each lesson ends with a fun-to-do take-along page that encourages kids to keep the learning going at home. Scripture puzzles, crafts, recipes, games, Bible read-about-its, Mighty Memory Verse reinforcement, and more challenge kids through independent discovery and learning fun. *Purpose: To reinforce, review, and enrich the day's lesson and the Mighty Memory Verse.*

PLUS, in every Power Builder's book you'll discover these great features!

★ **WHIZ QUIZZES!** At the end of each section is a reproducible Whiz Quiz to gently, yet effectively, assess what has been learned. Completed by kids in about five minutes at the end of lessons 3, 6, 9, and 12, the Whiz Quiz is a nonthreatening and fun measuring tool to allow teachers, kids, and parents to actually see what has been learned in the prior weeks. When kids complete each Whiz Quiz, consider presenting them a collectible surprise such as a vase and silk flowers that represent how God's joy is growing and flowering in their lives. For example, after the first Whiz Quiz, present each child with a small bud vase. After the next Whiz Quiz, present a red silk flower. Then use blue and yellow flowers for lessons 9 and 12.

When the book is complete, kids will have an entire bouquet to remind them of the way God's joy flowers in our lives even in the most difficult of situations. Kids will love the cool reminders of the lessons and their accomplishments! Be sure to keep children's completed Whiz Quiz pages in folders to present to kids at the end of the book or at the end of the year, in combination with other Whiz Quizzes from different books in the Power Builders Series.

★ **LESSON 13 REVIEW!** The last lesson in *Joy Builders* is an important review of all that's been learned, applied, accomplished, and achieved during the past twelve weeks. Kids will love the lively review games, action songs, unique review tools, and celebratory feel of this special lesson!

★ **SCRIPTURE STRIPS!** At the back of the book, you'll discover every Mighty Memory Verse and extra-challenge verse that appears in *Joy Builders*. These reproducible Scripture strips can be copied and cut apart to use over and over for crafts, games, cards, bookmarks, and other fun and fabulous "you-name-its"! Try gluing these strips to long Formica chips to make colorful, clattery key chains that double as super Scripture reviews!

★ **TEACHER FEATURE!** Discover timeless teaching tips and hints, hands-on help, and a whole lot more in this mini teacher workshop. Every book in the Power Builders Series offers a unique Teacher Feature that helps leaders understand and teach through issues such as discipline, prayer, Scripture memory, and more. The Teacher Feature in *Joy Builders* is "Presenting Memorable Messages."

God bless you as you teach with patience, love, and this powerful resource to help launch kids into another century of love, learning, and serving God! More POWER to you!

PRESENTING MEM-ORABLE MESSAGES

Think for a moment about the numbers of quick messages, kids sermons, devotions, and lesson activities you present to your kids in Sunday school, children's church, VBS, or other kids programs during the year. Let's say you present about five messages in a typical week. Doing a bit of simple math, this translates into 260 messages a year if you teach one age level of kids. And if you team-teach and have multiple age levels, the numbers climb even higher! Messages, devotions, five-minute kids' sermons, and lesson activities are vital to children's Christian education, but unfortunately most kids' messages have a bit too much in common. They're overworked, well-worn, and quite possibly ho-hum dull. It's not the truths these messages contain that begin to wear thin, but the presentation of the messages that need a boost to jump start them into kids' hearts and lives. So how can messages, no matter how short, be presented in clever, kid-pleasing ways and still get the point across memorably? By using your SMARTS! Check out the following acronym for SMARTS, then read on to discover how to make memorable messages come alive in your classroom the SMART way!

S—surprise

M—manipulate

A—assess

R—relate

T—tie to theme

S—summarize

SMARTS

USING SURPRISE OR SUSPENSE. All forms of media, from television commercials to fiction books and movies, know well that there is a slim window of time in which to engage an audience. If the presentation isn't attention-grabbing, it simply won't hold any interest for an audience. Message times for kids, with their lightning-fast attention spans, are no less challenging. The challenge becomes how to kick off messages in an engaging way that will hold kids' interests until learning has taken place. We can take valuable hints from outside media sources and recognize that the elements of *surprise* and *suspense* are two powerful tools to lock in interest from the start.

Beginning a message or devotion with an eye-popping presentation, slick trick, or other surprising demonstration or visual "hook" stimulates kids' interest and focuses their attention on what is unfolding. How does this work? Let's say you would like to present a message on Jesus as the light of the world. Beginning your message time with glow-in-the-dark sugar cubes from a kids' science experiments handbook is ever so much more clever and attention-grabbing than simply holding up a flashlight or unlit candle to get kids talking about light. Besides being surprising and unusual, a wow-'em beginning like glow-in-the-dark sugar cubes makes the entire message glowingly memorable long after class is over.

Creating an element of surprise or suspense isn't as difficult as you might imagine. Check out libraries for a great selection of Mr. Wizard-type science books for kids and see what amazing stunts you can match to themes you'll be presenting. Other great resources are easy-to-do books of tricks and sleight-of-hand demonstrations. For example, disappearing dimes can pique kids' interest as they begin to discover that God seeks the lost. Another great place to begin planning memorable messages is with kids' cookbooks. Look for ways to begin message times with clever, attention-getting demonstrations and devices, and you'll have your kids hooked in no time! But what about after you have their full attention? Read on!

USING MANIPULATIVES OR MAKING CRAFTS. Studies have shown that we retain only about 10 percent of what we hear but nearly 70 percent of what we *do*. Hands-on experiences and concrete manipulatives in conjunction with discussion and exploration of a theme help lock away learning. If messages for kids are to be memorable as well as instructive, it's important to implement a strategy that includes concrete manipulatives. Making crafts that emphasize the theme is a fun way to underscore what's being taught. Kids will readily remember that things happen in God's time if they're involved in making cool Hebrew calendars. Or imagine the enrichment fun if kids discover the importance of God's Word by making stained-glass Scripture windows! Combining craft projects and memorable messages makes each moment count in tight classroom schedules. Instead of a dull message time and an added craft project, why not combine the two for a powerful presentation?

Another way to implement manipulatives is through edible enrichment of themes. Letting kids prepare a batch of haroseth to spread on crackers is a sure-fire way to lock in the importance of being ready for God's call any time or place. Check out kids' cookbooks for fun-to-prepare recipes that match upcoming message themes.

ASSESSING AND ASSIMILATING TRUTHS. After you've captured kids' attention and have offered concrete ways to lock in learning, don't forget to add a brief, pointed discussion time during which kids can pull together what they're learning and share their thoughts. Small-group discussions and having partners share insights help kids put into words what they're learning, even as it strengthens communication skills and relationships. Brief question-and-answer times or Bible verse hunts make this important time exciting for kids.

HELPING KIDS RELATE. Making sure that kids recognize the relevance of the truths they're learning is just as important as assessing and assimilating what they're actually learning during your message time. Make sure your messages are directly relevant to kids' lives and offer them "take-home" tools to put to use right away. Exploring how sacrifices were made in Old Testament times is fascinating, but kids need to know ways we can give to God through our lives today. Always draw themes and messages back to kids' lives for the present and help kids discover how learning God's truths today impacts their faith tomorrow.

TYING IT ALL INTO THEMES. Memorable messages have easy-to-remember themes that accompany, enrich, or reinforce themes of lessons you're covering. Be careful to plan accordingly so you don't present a *message* about loyalty with a *lesson* that actually focuses on forgiveness. Dissimilar themes aren't easily recalled and tend to become fragmented in kids' minds. If you're learning about forgiveness, stick to themes such as God's grace, Jesus' forgiveness, or forgiving others. A bit of early planning can go miles in helping you coordinate themes with powerful messages that kids can easily remember and put to use in their lives.

SUMMARIZING TRUTHS. As important as how you begin a memorable message is how you bring the message to a close. Bring closure to messages by recapping what's been presented. A good tool is to repeat the beginning demonstration or invite kids to take turns presenting any cool tricks or presentations. Restating the message theme in a concise manner will help kids summarize what they've learned. Inviting kids to lead a short prayer at the close of message time is another good way to bring closure. As with any term paper, prayer, or letter, a good beginning, a meaty body, and a solid closing help make the message three-dimensional as well as memorable!

Presenting memorable messages can be as fun for leaders as it is life-changing for kids. So use your SMARTS! A bit of planning, preparation, and imagination can make the difference between a kids' devotion or sermon that sinks and one that soars into their hearts!

PARENT PAGE NEWSLETTER

Dear Parent:

Your child is about to embark on a wonderful exploration of the joy we have through Jesus and his awesome love! In the book *Joy Builders,* children will discover that true joy comes from Jesus and his love, that our joy is made complete by obeying Christ's command to love others, that joy from Jesus lasts forever and is powerfully different from everyday happiness or gladness, plus much more. You can help in your child's learning process by:

★ joining in the fun of the take-home Power Pages,
★ helping your child learn the Mighty Memory Verses,
★ reading Bible verses on joy and how we rejoice in Jesus,
★ portraying a positive role-model for joy even during "joyless" times, and
★ inquiring how your child is doing on the Whiz Quiz reviews.

Being a part of your child's growing spiritual experience brings wonderful opportunities to share your own faith and love for God. God bless you as you discover the endless joy that comes from loving Jesus, others, and our perfect Father in heaven!

> *You have made known to me the path of life;*
> *you will fill me with joy in your presence.*
> *Psalm 16:11*

JOY THROUGH JESUS' TEACHING

Whoever gives heed to
instruction prospers, and blessed is
he who trusts in the LORD.
Proverbs 16:20

JESUS' SUPER SERMON

Jesus' lessons give us joy, truth, and love!

Matthew 4:23, 24; 5:1-12
Mark 6:6
Luke 10:21

SESSION SUPPLIES

★ Bibles
★ gift wrap & balloons
★ napkins & paper cups
★ simple party foods (see Power Focus)
★ photocopies of the Bee-Attitudes (page 123)
★ markers & scissors
★ glue & tape
★ honeycomb-shaped cereal
★ foam cups & thin wire
★ a photocopy of the If & Then strips (page 16)
★ photocopies of the Power Page! (page 19)

MIGHTY MEMORY VERSE

Whoever gives heed to instruction prospers, and blessed is he who trusts in the LORD. Proverbs 16:20

SESSION OBJECTIVES

During this session, children will
★ realize that Jesus is our perfect teacher
★ discover that Jesus taught us God's truth
★ explore how Jesus' lessons bring us joy
★ learn that Jesus taught with God's wisdom and power

BIBLE BACKGROUND

School days, school days ... what are your memories of being in school? Did you enjoy the learning and the challenges to understand and apply that learning in your life? Many adults often voice the sentiment that they miss going to school and the learning they accomplished. But when we stop to remember the best teacher we've ever had, we realize that *Jesus* is still at work teaching, leading, and guiding the lessons of our lives! And the best part? Jesus' lessons continue on as long as we're willing to be teachable!

Ask kids what they think about school, and you'll probably receive a groan in response. But under all the groans and gripes, most kids enjoy being challenged and seeing the progress they make through learning. In spite of their occasional protests, kids are open to discovery and are good at putting what they learn to use in their lives. So use this delightful lesson about the Beatitudes to help kids discover the joy of learning about Jesus and his powerful, sensible, life-changing lessons.

POWER FOCUS

Before class, set up a quick party table and decorations. Cover a table in festive gift wrap and set out colorful napkins and paper cups. Blow up a balloon for each child and tape the balloons around the room. Finally, plan to serve simple party foods such as chilled apple juice and glazed donuts with bright sprinkles on top or festive fruit parfaits served in clear plastic cups.

Welcome kids to class and let them know you're happy to see them. Ask kids to name things that bring them great joy. Examples might include their families, special pets, favorite sports, good friends, church, sunny days, and God. Encourage kids to explain what makes something or someone a joy. Say: **Many things and people bring us a special happiness we call "joy." Families, friends, music, and hobbies can bring us joy. So can special parties and celebrations! Let's celebrate the joy we find in one another and in learning about Jesus with a joyful party in a jiffy!**

Invite kids to share in a kick-off party for *Joy Builders* and let them enjoy the tasty party treats and colorful surroundings. As kids munch their goodies, say: **Joy and rejoicing are mentioned over and over in the Bible—especially in the New Testament and when we talk about Jesus. That's because Jesus is the one who brings us true, lasting joy. For the next several weeks we'll be learning about joy through Jesus and why this kind of joy can never be taken away. We'll discover that Jesus brings us joy in many ways, and one of those ways is through his teachings. Today we'll explore how Jesus' teachings bring us joy through God's truth and obeying his Word. But first, let's get buzzing so we can make cool bees to help us learn about Jesus' joy.**

Have kids clean up the party area.

THE MIGHTY MESSAGE

Before class, photocopy the Bee-Attitudes from page 123 for each child. You'll also need to collect thin wire, foam cups, markers, scissors, glue, tape, and honeycomb-shaped cereal. Cut the wire into nine 5-inch lengths for each child.

Invite kids to form pairs or trios and hand everyone a foam cup, a copy of the Bee-Attitude bees, and nine pieces of wire. Have kids quickly cut out the bee patterns by cutting loosely around the outlines. As kids work, say: **Jesus is the greatest teacher we'll ever have! He loved to teach others about God's truths, how to obey God, and how to love each other. The Bible tells us that Jesus went from village to village teaching crowds of people.** Read aloud Matthew 4:23, 24; 22:33; and Mark 6:6.

When the bees are cut out, say: **One day when Jesus saw a very large crowd, he climbed a mountainside so he could teach them. Jesus taught a series of important truths that we call the "Beatitudes." The Beatitudes teach us the *attitudes* Jesus wants us to have and the ways he wants us to *be*. Let's use these cute bees to help us learn the attitudes we're to have and the ways Jesus wants us to be.**

Read each Beatitude from Matthew 5:3-12. After each Beatitude is read, have kids find that bee pattern and tape a piece of wire to it. Poke the wires through the tops of the foam cups. Bend the wires inside the cups and tape the ends in place inside the cups. Discuss what each Beatitude means and why it's an important attitude or way to "be" for Jesus. If there's time, let kids quickly color their bees before attaching the wires. When all nine bees are "buzzing" around each beehive cup, ask:

★ **In what ways do the Beatitudes help us live happily with others? with God?**

★ **How does Jesus' teaching bring us joy? truth? powerful guidance?**

★ **Why is it important to obey Jesus' teaching?**

Have kids glue honeycomb-shaped cereal to the foam cups to make them look like beehives. (If time is running short, simply use yellow markers to

POWER POINTERS

Assemble a large beehive on the wall or bulletin board, using empty egg cartons as honeycomb. Have kids cut large bees to fly around the hive, then write the Beatitudes on the bees.

color the hives.) Then read aloud Matthew 5:12 once again and say: **Jesus' teaching makes us want to rejoice and be glad because the lessons we learn from him help draw us closer to God and others. That's joyful learning, isn't it? Let's play a lively, joy-filled game to help us learn Jesus' Beatitudes even better. You'll need your buzzing beehives to play.**

THE MESSAGE IN MOTION

Before class, make one photocopy of the If & Then strips from page 16. Cut the strips apart on the dotted lines and keep one If & Then strip to read to kids. Separate the first halves of the remaining strips (the "If" portions) from the endings (the "Then" portions).

Set the eight "Then" strips at one end of the room. Have kids hold their beehives from the Mighty Message, form two groups of "bees," and stand at the opposite end of the room from the game strips. Hand each group four "If" strips. Finally, place several objects in the center of the room to make an obstacle course for the pretend bees to fly around.

Explain that in this lively relay-type game, kids will take turns "flying" their bees around the obstacles. They'll travel to gather a game strip and fly it back to their group's "hive" (starting place). If the strip completes one of their four game strips, tape the strips together to complete the verse. (Read the strip halves you kept back as an example.) If the strip is not a match, it must be returned to the pile at the opposite end of the room and another strip collected and flown back. Encourage kids to use their beehives to help match the words. Continue until all the strips have been taped together and all the verses assembled.

When the eight strips are assembled, say: **Whew! I saw a lot of busy bees at work learning the Beatitudes! Did you know that the Beatitudes can be thought of as "if and then" verses? The first portion of each Beatitude is the "if" portion, and the last part is the "then" portion. For example, "If we're merciful, *then* we'll be shown mercy." Now let's see if you can read your group's game strips as "ifs and thens."**

When the strips have been read, say: **What a joyous feeling to know that *if* we learn and obey Jesus' teachings, *then* we'll rejoice and be glad because of our reward in heaven! Let's increase our joy even more by beginning to learn a new Mighty Memory Verse that teaches us about learning from Jesus.**

IF we're poor in spirit,
THEN we'll have the kingdom of heaven.

IF we mourn,
THEN we'll be comforted.

IF we're meek,
THEN we'll inherit the earth.

IF we hunger and thirst for righteousness,
THEN we'll be filled.

IF we're merciful,
THEN we'll be shown mercy.

IF we're pure in heart,
THEN we'll see God.

IF we're peacemakers,
THEN we'll be called children of God.

IF we're persecuted for righteousness,
THEN the kingdom of heaven is ours.

IF we're insulted because of Jesus,
THEN we'll be blessed.

SUPER SCRIPTURE

Before class, write Proverbs 16:20 on a sheet of newsprint. Circle the words "prosper" and "blessed." Tape the paper to the wall or a door for kids to see. You may also wish to write the words and hand signs to the song in this activity on newsprint and tape the newsprint to a wall for kids to read.

Have kids repeat Proverbs 16:20 echo-style several times. Then say: **This powerful verse teaches us that learning is useful only when it is heeded or obeyed. When we learn and obey what is taught, and when we trust in God, we'll receive two wonderful gifts from the Lord: prosperity and blessings. Now you can see how learning brings us joy! Today we've been learning God's Word, which brings us joy. So let's learn a new song about the joy we have in the Lord and his teaching.**

Teach kids how to sign the letters in the word *joy* by using the diagrams in the margin. Then sing the following song to the tune of Old MacDonald, jumping in the air each time you sing the word *joy*. Follow the other actions in italics to complete this lively, joy-filled song.

JOY SONG

There is joy down in my heart, (point to your heart)
And Jesus put it there! (point upward)
Joy that cannot fade away (shake your finger "no")
And follows everywhere! (turn around in place)
J-O-Y, sign it high— (sign the letters for "joy" two times)
Jump for joy and give high fives! (jump, then give high fives)
There is joy down in my heart, (point to your heart)
And Jesus put it there! (point upward)

After singing, say: **What a fun, joyful song! And you've learned how to express the word** *joy* **through singing, talking, and spelling it in sign language. Now we can express our joy in Jesus' teachings through prayer.** Keep the words to Proverbs 16:20 and the Joy Song to use next week.

A **POWERFUL** PROMISE

Have kids sit in a circle holding their beehives. Say: **Today we've discovered that Jesus is our perfect teacher who instructs us in God's truths. We've learned that there are nine Beatitudes to teach us the attitudes we're to have and the ways Jesus wants us to be. We also began learning a new Mighty Memory Verse that says** (lead kids in repeating Proverbs 16:20), **"Whoever gives heed to instruction prospers, and blessed is he who trusts in the LORD."**

Hold up the Bible and say: **God's Word teaches us how to be joy-filled and tells us where joy lies. The Beatitudes help us know how to live in joyous ways. Let's offer a prayer thanking the Lord for the Beatitudes and the joy they bring us when we obey them. When we get to the appropriate part, we'll go around the circle, and you can read one of the Beatitudes from your bees.** Pray: **Dear Lord, we thank you for the joy your teaching brings. Please help us trust you and your Word as we obey your teachings. Thank you for the Beatitudes that teach us ...** (read the Beatitudes around the circle). Close with a corporate "amen."

Read aloud Luke 10:21, then end with this responsive good-bye:

Leader: **May the joy of Jesus' teachings be with you.**

Children: **And also with you!**

Distribute the Power Page! take-home papers as kids are leaving. Thank children for coming and encourage them to review the Beatitudes from their beehives during the week as they seek to obey them every day.

POWER PAGE!

IFs AND THENs

We know that IF we love Jesus, THEN we'll find joy. But Jesus taught us other powerful IFS & THENS. Use your Bible to match up the IFS & THENS from the Beatitudes in Matthew.

IF . . .   **THEN . . .**

we're merciful
(5:7)   we'll be
                                         comforted

we're peace-
makers (5:9)   we'll see
                                         God

we mourn
(5:4)   we'll inherit
                                         the earth

we're pure in
heart (5:8)   we'll be
                                         shown mercy

we're meek   we'll be called
(5:5)   children of God

A-Buzz with JOY!

Make this buzzy wind chime to remind you how joy from Jesus is music to our hearts!

You'll need:
- ★ small clay pot
- ★ pottery paints
- ★ chenille wire
- ★ 3-inch nail
- ★ ribbon
- ★ 3 jingle bells
- ★ white craft felt
- ★ tacky craft glue

Directions:
(1) Paint the clay pot and add a cute face. Let the pot dry overnight. **(2)** Tie a 10-inch ribbon to the center of the nail. Tie 5-inch lengths of ribbon to each bell and hang the bells from the nail. **(3)** Twist chenille wires to the middle of the nail. Push the long ribbon and wires up through the hole in the top of the pot. **(4)** Glue on felt wings.

High & LOW

Fill in the missing high, low, and in-between letters to complete Proverbs 16:20.

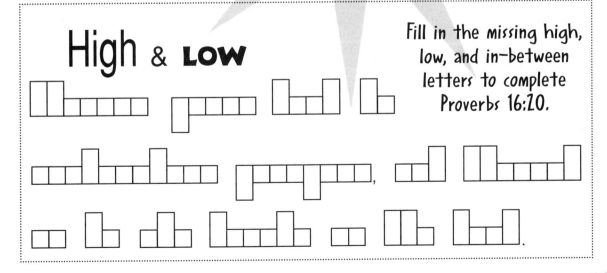

FOUNDATION OF JOY

Joy is found when we build our lives on Jesus.

Isaiah 28:16
Luke 6:47-49
1 Corinthians 3:11

SESSION SUPPLIES

★ Bibles
★ craft feathers
★ toothpicks
★ bricks
★ tacky craft glue
★ cotton swabs
★ glitter or sequins
★ photocopies of the Scripture strip for Proverbs 16:20 (page 127)
★ photocopies of the Power Page! (page 27)

MIGHTY MEMORY VERSE

Whoever gives heed to instruction prospers, and blessed is he who trusts in the LORD. Proverbs 16:20
(For older kids, add in 1 Corinthians 3:11: "For no one can lay any foundation other than the one already laid, which is Jesus Christ.")

SESSION OBJECTIVES

During this session, children will
★ discover that Jesus teaches on what to build our lives and faith
★ learn that Jesus is our only true foundation
★ realize that prayer is part of a foundation of faith
★ understand that joy comes from lives focused on Jesus

BIBLE BACKGROUND

"Early to bed, and early to rise ..." "A penny saved is a penny earned"—Benjamin Franklin went a long way in bringing "everyday wisdom" to our culture with his witty sayings for life lessons with sensible solutions. But Franklin's wisdom is short-lived in our temporal world and doesn't prepare us for eternity or show us the way to our heavenly Father. Discovering true wisdom that's just as sensible, often as witty, and incomparable in truth, one need look no further than the Bible! Jesus spent his short life bringing us everyday wisdom and teaching us where and how to build our lives—both for today and tomorrow.

Although *Poor Richard's Almanac* sits on sands that eventually wash away, Christ's wisdom in the Bible stands on solid rock!

Most kids readily admit that they're too young to be considered wise and, in turn, look to their parents, grandparents, and teachers for wisdom and guidance. Fortunately, if words of wisdom are put in terms kids can truly grasp, they tend to accept and follow the guidance. Isn't it wonderful that Jesus gave us such clear examples of wisdom even kids can hold on to? The wise and foolish builders are wonderful examples of where and how to build our lives and help kids visualize the consequences of wrong choices.

POWER focus

Before class, collect a bag of craft feathers, a box of toothpicks, and a brick for each child. You'll be using the bricks throughout this lesson and decorating them as cornerstones. Small bricks will work fine, but if you prefer, use pre-poured cement stepping stones.

Set the bricks, feathers, and toothpicks in three separate piles around the room. Welcome kids to class and ask if they're ready to do a little building. Have kids form three construction teams and assign each group a pile of building materials. Say: **Remember the story of the Three Little Pigs and how they built their houses out of different materials? We'll attempt to build houses as well. You'll have three minutes to build any kind of house you'd like. At the end of three minutes, we'll travel around and give the structures the ol' huff-n-puff test!**

Encourage kids to communicate and work together in their groups. At the end of three minutes, call time. Have kids visit each building site and test the sturdiness with the huff-n-puff test: attempting to blow over the buildings. The brick building will be the only structure that remains unchanged. Say: **When we're doing any building, it obviously makes a difference what materials we build with and where we build. Foundations must be strong and firm, steady and strong to withstand trials and tests. Jesus taught us a lot about firm foundations and where we're to build our lives so our joy and faith can withstand trials and tests.**

Today we'll discover Jesus' special blueprints for building our lives in joyous, powerful ways. We'll see how joy comes from building firm faith and that with a strong foundation built on Jesus, our joy can stand strong forever! Let's explore how and where Jesus teaches us to build

21

our lives. You'll need these building materials to help. Hand each child a craft feather, a toothpick, and a brick.

THE **MIGHTY** MESSAGE

Before class, check to see if your church building has a cornerstone. If so, plan to show this special stone to your kids.

Have kids scatter around the room so they have space to move as they act out the parable of the wise and foolish builders. Say: **Place your building materials on the floor for right now. Did you**

POWER POINTERS

Invite a church leader in to visit with kids about what it means to dedicate their lives to Jesus. Encourage questions, and end with a prayer thanking Jesus for being our cornerstone.

know that Jesus received great joy through teaching, especially children? Listen to what Luke 10:21 says. "At that time, Jesus, full of joy through the Holy Spirit, said, 'I praise you, Father, Lord of heaven and earth, because you have hidden these things from the wise and learned, and revealed them to little children. Yes, Father, for this was your good pleasure.'" Isn't that neat? Jesus had joy teaching children because he knew you would hear his words, learn from them, and receive great joy. And one of the things Jesus taught was how and where to build our lives. Listen to this parable, or story, that Jesus told. Follow along as we act out the parable of the wise and foolish builders. When you hear the word *foolish*, **wave the feathers and hold up the toothpicks. When you hear the word** *wise*, **stand on your bricks.**

Retell the parable from Luke 6:47-49 and follow the actions. **Once there were two builders—one who was** *wise* **and one who was** *foolish*. **The** *foolish* **builder built his house on sand. What do you think happened when floods came? The foundation snapped . . .** (snap the toothpicks in half), **and the house just whooshed away!** (Blow the feathers in the air.) **But the *wise* builder dug down deep to find solid rock.** (Make digging motions.) **That *wise* man built his house on solid rock to give it a firm foundation. How very *wise* he was! For when the rains came, his house stood firm and couldn't be washed away. And the man's joy from his wisdom couldn't be washed away either!** (Stand on the bricks and cheer.) Have kids sit on their bricks, then ask:

★ **What did the wise man do because he was so wise?**

★ **How does a firm foundation help buildings stand strong and firm?**

★ **In what ways is Jesus like a strong, firm foundation on which to build our lives?**

Say: **Jesus told this parable so we would learn that where and how we build our lives is very important. If we choose to build our lives on flimsy things such as money, lies, or empty fame, we'll end up like the foolish man who built his house on the sand. But when we choose Jesus as the foundation and base for our lives, we'll stand firm and joyous like the house on the rock!** Ask:

★ **What can we do to make Jesus the foundation on which we build our lives?**

★ **How does faith help us build a strong foundation? How does prayer help? obeying the Lord? learning God's Word?**

Say: **There are many ways to strengthen our foundation being built on Jesus. Praying, obeying God, learning God's Word, and having faith are powerful ways. Let's write those ways on our bricks to remind us how to build our lives on Jesus.**

Have kids use cotton swabs and tacky craft glue to write the following words on the four sides of their bricks: *obey, pray, faith,* and *God's Word.* Then sprinkle glitter or press sequins into the wet glue.

Say: **Now let's discover the most important stone in any foundation and who we want as the cornerstone of our lives and our joy!** Keep the glue, glitter or sequins, and bricks handy to use in the next activity.

THE MESSAGE IN MOTION

Say: **Most buildings have a very special stone in their foundation. It's called a "cornerstone," and it is put there with the date on which the building was dedicated for use.** (If your church has a cornerstone, view it now.) **The Bible speaks of a special cornerstone that is to be the cornerstone of our lives. Listen to the following verses. When you know who that cornerstone is, put your hand on your heart.** Invite volunteers to read aloud 1 Corinthians 3:11; Isaiah 28:16; and Ephesians 2:20. Have kids tell that Jesus is our cornerstone. Then say: **Jesus is that special, all-powerful cornerstone we want to build our lives on. It brings me such joy and comfort to know that Jesus is my cornerstone and the firm foundation of my faith and life!**

Cornerstones on buildings usually state the date on which a building was dedicated and could be used. In a similar way, we can dedicate our lives to Jesus as our cornerstone to show that we're willing to be used by him. We'll add today's date to our cornerstone bricks to show we want to dedicate our lives to making Jesus our firm foundation to build on today and for the rest of our lives.

Have kids use tacky craft glue and glitter or sequins to make the date on the tops of their bricks. Use abbreviations for months or write the date using numbers and slash marks or hyphens.

When the stones are complete, have kids stand beside their cornerstones and lead them in the following prayer. **Dear Lord, the joy we feel in making you the cornerstone of our lives is awesome! From this day on, we will celebrate you as the cornerstone of our lives and will strengthen this powerful foundation of faith and joy by praying to you, obeying you, and learning your Word. We love you, Lord. Amen.**

Say: **What joy there is in making Jesus the cornerstone and foundation of our lives! Let's express our joy by singing the song we learned last week. Find a partner to sing with and give high fives to.** Lead kids in singing the Joy Song to the tune of Old MacDonald and in doing the accompanying motions. (See page 17 to review how to spell *joy* in sign language.)

JOY SONG

There is joy down in my heart, (point to your heart)
And Jesus put it there! (point upward)

Joy that cannot fade away (shake your finger "no")
And follows everywhere! (turn around in place)
J-O-Y, sign it high— (sign the letters for "joy" two times)
Jump for joy and give high fives! (jump, then give high fives)
There is joy down in my heart, (point to your heart)
And Jesus put it there! (point upward)

Say: **Wow! Look at the smiles on your faces! Isn't it great to know that Jesus put that joy in your hearts? One way we can strengthen our foundation of faith is by learning God's Word. Let's review the Mighty Memory Verse we started learning last week as we strengthen our foundations.**

SUPER SCRIPTURE

Be sure the words to Proverbs 16:20 are still taped to the wall from last week. Photocopy the Scripture strip for Proverbs 16:20 from page 127, one for each child. If you have older kids and plan to learn the extra-challenge verse, write the words to 1 Corinthians 3:11 on newsprint and tape it to the wall or door.

Have kids repeat Proverbs 16:20 three times aloud, then invite kids to take turns covering up portions of the verse and challenging friends to repeat the verse. (If you have older kids, introduce the extra-challenge verse at this time.) Then say: **This verse teaches us that obeying Jesus' teaching and trusting in the Lord helps us prosper in life and receive God's blessings. Think for a moment about having Jesus as our cornerstone and foundation.** Ask:

★ **In what ways does giving heed to instruction, or obeying Jesus' teaching, help us build a strong foundation of faith?**

★ **How does trusting the Lord make our foundation even stronger?**

Hand each child a Scripture strip of Proverbs 16:20. Glue the strips to the bottoms of the bricks. Then say: **One way to make Jesus our cornerstone is to listen to and obey his teachings. In this way, we'll find joy that can't be taken away because we're like the wise man who built on a firm foundation. The wise man built on rock-solid rock—we can build on rock-solid Scripture! The truths of God's Word and obeying Jesus' teaching strengthen our foundation, but so does powerful prayer. Let's offer a prayer thanking Jesus for the joy we receive through**

being wise and building our lives on him. Keep the newsprint verse to use next week.

A **POWERFUL** PROMISE

Have kids place their cornerstones beside them. Say: **We've been learning that Jesus is our only foundation and cornerstone. We've discovered ways to strengthen our foundation of faith, and we've reviewed our Mighty Memory Verse that teaches us to heed Jesus' instruction and trust in the Lord. In these ways, our joy will be great and can never be washed away.**

Hold up the Bible and say: **Scripture teaches us that the way to find real joy is through building our lives on Jesus. It also teaches us that obeying the Lord, praying, keeping our faith strong, and learning God's Word build that foundation even stronger. Earlier we dedicated our lives to Jesus, making him the cornerstone of our lives. Now we'll pass the Bible to one another, and when you receive it, you can say to Jesus, "You're my foundation strong and true; the cornerstone of my life is you!"** After everyone has had a turn to hold the Bible, close with a corporate "amen."

Read aloud Colossians 2:6, 7. Then end with this responsive good-bye:

Leader: **May Jesus remain your joyous foundation.**

Children: **And also yours!**

Distribute the Power Page! take-home papers as kids are leaving. Remind kids to take their cornerstones home to remind them of their promise to keep Jesus the firm foundation of their lives.

POWER PAGE!

ROCK OF AGES

Fill in the words after the clues, then complete the puzzle below.

another word
for rock
S _ _ _ _
        2   5

tall heap
of stone
M _ _ _ _ _
     8

square building
blocks
B _ _ _ _ _
   6 1 7

large, round
rock
B _ _ _ _ _ _
   9   11 3

what we
build on
F _ _ _ _ _ _ _ _
    4   10

We want Jesus to be our

_ _ _ _ _ _ _ _ _ _ _
1 2 3 4 5 6 7 8 9 10 11

Key Stone

Make a cool Key Stone as a secret hiding place for notes, keys, or special trinkets!

Mold **gray self-hardening clay** into a large stone shape. Use your **fingers** to press a 2-inch-by-1-inch dent in the bottom of the stone. (Make sure it's big enough to hold a house key!) Let your Key Stone harden for several days until it's completely dry. Cut a flat 2½-by-1½-inch piece of **plastic** from a milk or detergent jug. Attach the plastic to the stone's dent with a tiny **screw**. (The plastic will be a sliding cover to hold the key inside.) Place your Key Stone on a desk or **shellac** it to use outside your door to hold a spare key!

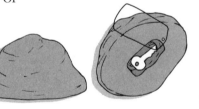

SCRIPTURE SCRAMBLER

Unscramble the words in the word bank to complete Proverbs 16:20.

_ _ _ _ _ _ _ _ _ _   _ _

_ _ _ _ _ _ _ _ _ _ _ _ _ _ _ _,

_ _ _ _ _ _ _ _ _ _ _ _ _ _ _ _ _ _ _

_ _ _ _ _ _ _ _ _ _ _ _ _ _.

WORD BANK

vegis	*ot*
deslesb	*nad*
reprosps	*bow*
struts	*si*
overWbe	*eb*
doLr	*ni*
debe	*bet*
tucrsitnino	

SERVING UP JOY

Jesus joyfully demonstrated servanthood.

Psalm 100:2
John 13:13-15
Romans 12:11-13; 14:18

SESSION SUPPLIES

★ Bibles
★ newspapers
★ two garbage sacks
★ clear plastic drinking bottles
★ pitcher & paper towels
★ permanent markers
★ clear liquid dish soap
★ lemon juice
★ foil confetti pieces
★ tape
★ photocopies of the Whiz Quiz (page 36) and the Power Page! (page 35)

MIGHTY MEMORY VERSE

Whoever gives heed to instruction prospers, and blessed is he who trusts in the LORD. Proverbs 16:20
(For older kids, add in 1 Corinthians 3:11: "For no one can lay any foundation other than the one already laid, which is Jesus Christ.")

SESSION OBJECTIVES

During this session, children will
★ learn that serving others and God brings joy
★ explore ways to serve others
★ discover how Jesus taught by example
★ understand that Jesus served with love and joy

BIBLE BACKGROUND

Just as a magnifying glass magnifies leaves so we can see the tiniest of details, serving others magnifies the joy we feel through Jesus' love! When Jesus became the servant to wash the feet of his disciples, he gave us all a powerful example of how to share the joy in our hearts with others in life-changing ways. Whether it's an encouraging word to an ill friend or offering to drive an elderly neighbor to the store, the joy we feel from giving of ourselves and through Christ's love is magnified within our hearts and within the hearts of the people we serve.

Can anything be more bubbly and full of smiles than a child on a serving mission? Kids love helping others and usually throw themselves into service projects with all their hearts and hands. And though they know Jesus helped others in many ways, it's often a surprise to learn that Jesus felt great *joy* in being a servant. After all, he is God's Son and our mighty, heavenly King! Use this lesson to help kids realize that Jesus drew great joy from serving others and wants us to receive that same joyous feeling from serving others too.

POWER FOCUS

Before class, wad up several newspapers worth of pages and scatter them around the floor, tables, shelves, and chairs. You'll also need small, clear plastic water bottles with the pull-up tops for drinking (or clear plastic bottles with lids). Collect a bottle and top for each child. Scatter the bottles on the floor with the newspapers. Place two garbage sacks at opposite ends of the room.

Welcome kids to class, then say: **Wow! There's quite a mess in here today! Find a partner, then I'll tell you how we can get this room clean and sparkling.** When kids have their partners, explain that in this cleanup activity, one partner picks up the trash and the other places it in a garbage sack. Designate one garbage bag as the newspaper sack and the other as the bottle bag. Tell kids they'll have three minutes to find all the newspapers and plastic bottles and place them in bags.

When the room is clean, have partners give each other high fives for a job well done. Say: **What a great cleaning job you all did! And I especially liked the way you worked together with such cheery attitudes.** Ask:

★ **Why was cleaning the room fun?**

★ **How was cleaning our room a way to serve the people in our class?**

★ **Do you think there is joy in serving and helping others? Explain.**

Say: **It was fun helping out to make our room clean and ready for learning. And you're right—there *is* joy in serving and helping. Jesus taught us about the joy of serving others through his own examples of helping, healing, and serving people. Today we'll explore the joy that comes from serving others and God. We'll learn about different ways we can joyously serve and how it pleases the Lord. And we'll review our Mighty Memory Verse that teaches us about the joy that comes from obeying the Lord and serving as he desires.**

Keep the plastic drinking bottles to use later in the lesson. Place the newspapers in a paper recycling bin or keep them to use for craft projects in the future.

THE **MIGHTY** MESSAGE

Before class, be sure you have a large, plastic pitcher and a place where kids can find water to fill the pitcher. (If there is no readily available sink, fill the pitcher before class.) You'll also need paper towels and colorful permanent markers.

Have kids sit in a group, then invite volunteers to serve by filling the pitcher with water that you'll need for this activity. Say: **Jesus spent his whole life serving others and God. He served in so many ways too. Who remembers some of the ways Jesus helped others or obeyed God?** Suggestions might include Jesus healing the ten lepers or the blind man, Jesus accepting Zacchaeus or the woman at the well, Jesus calming the storm or teaching others, and Jesus dying for our forgiveness. Ask:

★ **In what ways did Jesus demonstrate his love for us by serving others?**

★ **How did Jesus receive joy from helping others? serving God?**

Say: **Jesus taught us all about the joy of serving others. And he didn't just use words to teach us. Jesus taught us by example. In other words, Jesus** *showed* **us how to joyously serve and help others. He also taught us that, not only are we to serve with joy, but that joy and happiness come from serving. You might say that serving begins and ends with joy! Let's discover more about this truth by learning how Jesus served his disciples at the Last Supper. As you listen and watch, think of how joy helped Jesus serve his disciples.**

As you retell the story of how Jesus served through washing his disciples' feet (John 13:13-15), act out the story by washing the hand or foot of a child in class. Use a bit of water from the pitcher and the paper towels.

Say: **Jesus and his disciples were gathered for a special dinner. Jesus knew it would be his last supper on earth, and he wanted to use every moment to teach his disciples. When dinner was over, Jesus washed Peter's feet with cool water.** Wash a child's foot or hand with water. **Then Jesus dried Peter's feet with a towel.** Use a paper towel to dry off the

POWER POINTERS

Check out 101 Simple Service Projects Kids Can Do (Standard Publishing) for a super selection of quick ways to serve others. Kids can put their joy into action through serving as Jesus served!

child's hand or foot. **The disciples were amazed that Jesus would wash their feet. After all, he was their Master and God's Son! Then Jesus said** (read aloud John 13:13-15). **By joyfully serving his disciples, Jesus taught them that no one was too special or important to serve others. He taught us that we all are to serve one another and follow his example.** Ask:

★ **Why does Jesus want us to be servants?**

★ **How do we also serve the Lord when we serve others?**

★ **Do you think it brings Jesus joy when we serve others? Do you think it brings us joy? Explain.**

Say: **Jesus served his disciples with joy and love and demonstrated that we're all to be servants with joyous attitudes. And Jesus taught us that joy comes from serving as well.** Read Romans 14:18 aloud. **When we serve others, we serve God and also please him and give him joy. And that makes us feel joy, doesn't it? Let's use this water and the plastic bottles we cleaned up earlier to make a cool craft to serve others as we're reminded how Jesus served his disciples by washing their feet with joy and love.**

THE MESSAGE IN **MOTION**

Before class, collect shiny, precut foil confetti measuring cups and spoons, clear liquid dish soap, and lemon juice. Kids will be making awesome hand soap for their families to use when washing their hands.

Distribute the clear plastic drinking bottles. Have kids fill their bottles half full of water. Carefully add ½ cup of clear dishwashing soap, 1 tablespoon of lemon juice, and a small handful of shiny foil confetti bits. Replace the tops of the drinking bottles securely, then gently tip the bottles over a couple of times to mix the soap, water, and lemon juice.

Explain to kids that this special hand soap will clean their hands as it reminds them how Jesus taught us to serve one another with joy and love. Use permanent markers to write "Serve one another in love" on the plastic bottles. Then challenge kids to wash the hands of their family members as they explain about serving others in love and the joy that comes from serving.

Say: **We've been learning about the joy that comes from serving others, but what are ways we can serve? Let's read from the book of Romans to see if there are any clues.** Invite volunteers to read aloud Romans 12:11-13. Stop after each verse is read and list the ways we can serve, such as by being joyful in hope, faithful in prayer, and patient from verse 12. Then have kids name other ways to serve, such as through donating clothing or food to homeless shelters, reading the Bible to an elderly neighbor, or picking up trash on a school or church playground.

Say: **Just think of all the ways we can serve! Prayer, chores, speaking encouraging words, donating clothing, helping someone be patient, or showing hospitality are all powerful ways to serve God and others with joy. Another great way is through learning God's Word! Let's review our Mighty Memory Verse as we explore more about the joy that comes from serving others.**

SUPER SCRIPTURE

Be sure Proverbs 16:20 is still written on newsprint. Cut the newsprint into as many puzzle pieces as there kids in class. (If your class is very large, make two sets of puzzle pieces.)

Hand each child a puzzle piece. Repeat Proverbs 16:20 two times in unison, then challenge kids to construct the verse by fitting together their puzzle pieces and taping them together when the verse is completed correctly. If you have older kids who are learning the extra-challenge verse, review it at this time.

Say: **Let's see how well you've learned what this verse means. I'll read a sentence. If you agree with the sentence, give a thumbs-up sign. If you disagree, give a thumbs-down and explain why you disagree.**

★ *When we obey Jesus' teaching, we'll find joy.*

★ *If we obey Jesus' example, we'll please God.*

★ *It's not important to heed God's instruction.*

★ *We'll be blessed if we trust in Jesus.*

★ *Joy comes from money and being famous.*

★ *Joy comes from obeying Jesus and his teachings.*

Say: **One of the most powerful, sure-fire ways to find joy that never fades away is through obeying Jesus and following his teachings. Jesus taught us to serve others joyously and freely. And if we're to find true joy, we want to heed Jesus' instruction and serve others. Jesus taught us in words and through his examples of serving God and others. Jesus also taught through love and joy. Let's thank Jesus for his teachings that bring us such powerful joy that lasts forever.**

A POWERFUL PROMISE

Have kids sit in a circle. Say: **What a fun, joyous time we've had today learning about the joy that comes from serving others. We've discovered that serving begins and ends with joy and pleases the Lord. And we've reviewed our Mighty Memory Verse, which says** (repeat Proverbs 16:20 and the extra-challenge verse, if you've been learning it), **"Whoever gives heed to instruction prospers, and blessed is he who trusts in the LORD."**

Hold up the Bible and say: **God's Word teaches us about the joy that comes from serving others. Jesus promised to be with us always, and he serves us every day with love, truth, and help. Let's promise to obey Jesus' example of serving others and God in joy and love. We'll pass the Bible, and when you receive it, you can say, "I want to serve others in joy just as Jesus served."** When everyone has had a turn to hold the Bible, close with a corporate "amen."

Before kids leave, allow five or ten minutes to complete the Whiz Quiz from page 36. If you run out of time, be sure to do this page first thing next week. The Whiz Quiz is an invaluable tool that allows kids, teachers, and parents see what kids have learned in the previous three weeks.

Read aloud Psalm 100:2, then say: **Let's close by serving God with a joyous song!** Lead kids in singing the Joy Song to the tune of Old MacDonald.

JOY SONG

> ***There is joy down in my heart,*** *(point to your heart)*
> ***And Jesus put it there!*** *(point upward)*
> ***Joy that cannot fade away*** *(shake your finger "no")*
> ***And follows everywhere!*** *(turn around in place)*
> ***J-O-Y, sign it high—*** *(sign the letters for "joy" two times)*
> ***Jump for joy and give high fives!*** *(jump, then give high fives)*
> ***There is joy down in my heart,*** *(point to your heart)*
> ***And Jesus put it there!*** *(point upward)*

Then end with this responsive good-bye:

Leader: **May you serve one another in love and joy.**

Children: **And also you!**

Distribute the Power Page! take-home papers as kids are leaving. Remind kids to take home their hand soap as they remember the joy in serving God and others. Encourage kids to keep their promises to God this week.

POWER PAGE!

JOY from JESUS

Jesus teaches us there's joy in serving others. How did Jesus serve God and others? Read the verses, then draw lines to the matching hearts.

Matthew 12:22

Luke 7:48

Luke 5:16

Mark 6:6

Mark 10:21

forgave others

taught

loved others

prayed

healed others

Have-a-Heart

Want some serving fun with your family? Try this super serving idea and challenge your whole family to get involved.

Use permanent markers to decorate a solid-colored vinyl placemat with hearts. *Make* the hearts large enough to *write* in and *add* ways to serve, such as those in the Joy from Jesus activity to the left. *Set* the placemat in the center of your dining table. At mealtimes, have one family member *close* his or her eyes and *point* to a heart. See if you all can *serve* someone in that way for a day.

❤❤❤❤❤❤❤❤❤❤❤❤

CRACK THE CODE!

Use the key below to complete the **MIGHTY MEMORY VERSE**, Proverbs 16:20.

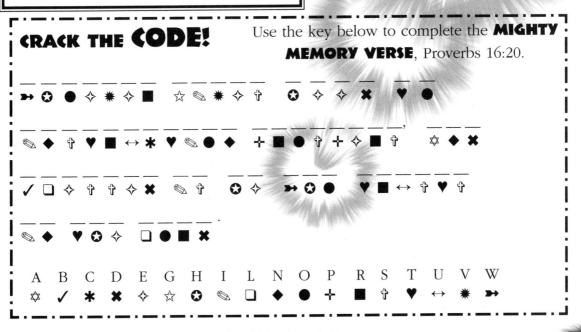

A	B	C	D	E	G	H	I	L	N	O	P	R	S	T	U	V	W
☆	✓	✳	✖	✧	☆	✪	✏	▢	◆	●	✛	■	✝	♥	↔	✱	➥

WHIZ QUIZ

Color in T (true) or F (false) to answer the questions.

➤ Jesus teaches God's truths. (T) (F)

➤ Jesus' teachings bring joy if we obey them. (T) (F)

➤ It is okay to build our lives on money. (T) (F)

➤ Prayer is part of a foundation in Jesus. (T) (F)

➤ Jesus was too important to serve others. (T) (F)

➤ Serving God and others begins and ends with joy. (T) (F)

AIM THE ARROWS

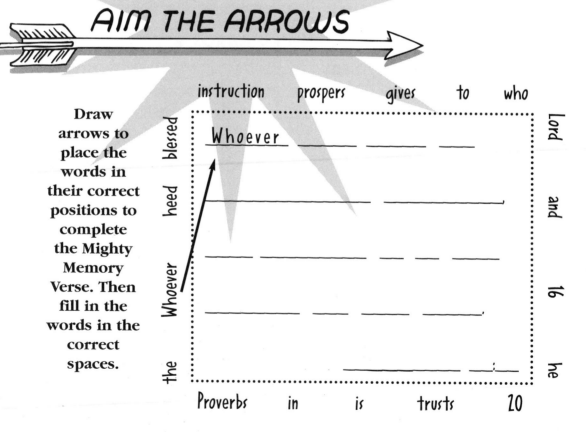

Draw arrows to place the words in their correct positions to complete the Mighty Memory Verse. Then fill in the words in the correct spaces.

instruction   prospers   gives   to   who

blessed   Whoever _____ _____ _____

heed   _____ _____

Whoever   _____ _____

the   _____

Lord   and   16   he

Proverbs   in   is   trusts   20

36

JOY THROUGH JESUS' LOVE

Above all, love each other
deeply, because love covers
over a multitude of sins.
1 Peter 4:8

ENOUGH TO GO AROUND

Our joy is complete when we love even the most unlovable people.

Matthew 5:43-47
Luke 19:1-10
Colossians 3:12-14

SESSION SUPPLIES

★ Bibles
★ kitchen scrubbies
★ tacky craft glue
★ googly craft eyes
★ chenille wires
★ construction paper
★ markers
★ scissors
★ newsprint
★ tape
★ photocopies of the Power Page! (page 45)

MIGHTY MEMORY VERSE

Above all, love each other deeply, because love covers over a multitude of sins. 1 Peter 4:8.

SESSION OBJECTIVES

During this session, children will
★ discover that Jesus loves all people
★ realize what "unconditional love" means
★ explore ways to be accepting and tolerant
★ learn that loving the "unlovable" brings us joy

BIBLE BACKGROUND

When was the last time you invited a homeless person to dinner or sent an encouraging card or flower to someone you don't get along with? To most of us, this would feel like asking for trouble. But Jesus went out of his way to include, accept, love, and encourage even the most unlovable people. Jesus knew it was easy to love those who already love us, so he gave us a special challenge. Jesus urged us to go beyond our comfort zones to reach out to the outcasts and "unlovables" around us. Jesus knew the precious truth that our joy is made complete when we love even our enemies and embrace those hardest to love.

Kids are all familiar with bullies, whether they're the neighborhood variety or those who stalk the playgrounds at school. Teasing, taunting, and being unkind are symptoms of hearts that hurt and grinding grudges against the world.

These are the people toughest to love. Ironically, however, they are also the ones who need our love most. Use this lively lesson to help kids realize that joy comes from loving, accepting, and forgiving those who reject us or hurt us the most.

POWER focus

Before class collect chenille wires, googly craft eyes, tacky craft glue, construction paper, scissors, and round kitchen scrubbies. These are the colorful, nylon netting balls used to scrub pots and pans. You'll need a scrubbie for each child plus one extra. Make an "Unlovey Scrubbie" to show kids by gluing on two googly eyes and a frowny paper mouth. Add bright antennae by wrapping a chenille wire around the scrubby ball.

Welcome kids warmly, then gather them around you. Hold up the Unlovey Scrubbie and say: **I'd like you to meet someone I brought to class today. This is Unlovey Scrubbie, and he's very prickly, cranky, and disagreeable. Unlovey Scrubbie complains and is mean and scratchy to others. He's not caring, he's very selfish, and he doesn't have any real friends. In fact, it's hard to love or even like Unlovey Scrubbie. Have you ever met someone like this?** Encourage kids to tell about people they know who may be tough to love or get along with, but tell kids not to mention any names.

Say: **Everyone knows someone who is tough to get along with and hard to love. But these are the people who often need our love the most! Let's make Unlovey Scrubbies to help us discover how to love even the most unlovable people around us.**

Let kids make their own Unlovey Scrubbies. As kids work, discuss character traits of people who are hard to love, such as they can be discouraging, mean spirited, bullyish, full of complaints, and selfish. Compare those traits with traits of someone easy to love and get along with.

When the scrubbies are done, say: **We've been learning about joy and how Jesus helps us find the way to real joy. Today we'll discover how loving others, even the most unlovable, makes our joy complete and great. We'll learn how Jesus loved hard-to-love people, and we'll explore ways we can be more accepting, loving, and kind to *all* people. Right now, let's discover how Jesus turned a cranky sourpuss whom no one loved into a giving man who was easy to love. We'll use our prickly Unlovey Scrubbies to help.**

THE MIGHTY MESSAGE

Gather kids in a circle and have them hold their scrubbies. Say: **When you hear me say the word *short,* touch your scrubbie to your toes. When I say the word *tall,* toss your scrubbie high in the air and catch it. If I ask a question during the story and you know the answer, wave your scrubbie in the air.**

Retell the following story of Zacchaeus from Luke 19:1-10 as kids follow along with their scrubbies.

Once there was a very *short* man. His name was Zacchaeus, and he was a tax collector. Even when people were *short* on money, Zacchaeus took it, because Zacchaeus was *short* on kindness and *tall* on selfishness. As a result, Zacchaeus was *short* on friends and love. Why do you think Zacchaeus was *short* on friends?

Allow kids to respond, then continue: **Now one day, *short* Zacchaeus heard Jesus was coming to town. He wanted to see this man whom everyone loved, but he was too *short* to see over the crowds. What could Zacchaeus do? Then he spied a very *tall* tree. Zacchaeus climbed that *tall* tree and hid in the leaves while he waited for Jesus to pass by.**

Suddenly Zacchaeus heard someone speaking to him. "Zacchaeus, come down. I'm going to your house today," said Jesus. Zacchaeus was amazed, but he climbed down the *tall* tree. The crowd was amazed too. Why would Jesus want to be with Zacchaeus when he was so unlovable?

POWER POINTERS

Have kids each choose someone who may be hard to love in their schools or neighborhoods to be their Secret Pals. Encourage kids to anonymously leave encouraging notes, Scripture verses, and small treats.

Zacchaeus shared his food with Jesus. And Jesus shared his love and forgiveness with Zacchaeus! Jesus showed *short,* cranky Zacchaeus the love he never had known. And Jesus forgave Zacchaeus for all the mean things he had done. Wow! Zacchaeus's love grew *tall* that day! He gave back the people's money and apologized to them. Zacchaeus discovered that when we're *short* on love and joy, Jesus shares his love in *tall* ways! Ask:

★ How did Jesus show love and acceptance to Zacchaeus?

★ Why did Zacchaeus change his ways?

★ In what ways did Zacchaeus change?

★ How can our love and acceptance help hard-to-love people?

Say: **Jesus knew Zacchaeus was cranky and very tough to love. But Jesus also knew that Zacchaeus needed love and acceptance. And just look how loving Zacchaeus changed his life! You know, the Bible tells us that it's easy to love the people who already love us. But we must try to love even the hard-to-love people around us.** Read aloud Matthew 5:43-47. Then ask:

★ Why is it important to love more than just those people who already love us?

★ How can we change someone's life by offering love, acceptance, and respect?

★ How can loving the hard-to-love bring them joy? bring us joy?

Say: **Hug your Unlovey Scrubbie to your cheek. It's scratchy and prickly, isn't it? But do you know what happens the more it is used and hugged and played with? It becomes softer and nicer to be near! That's how it is with people. When we love and show kindness to them, they become changed. It might take a while, but love makes a change that brings everyone joy. Let's play a game with our scrubbies and see if we can begin to see a change in them.**

THE MESSAGE IN MOTION

Have kids stand in a circle holding their scrubbies. Place the Unlovey Scrubbie you made earlier in the center of the circle. Have kids number off by fours. Explain that in this game kids will be naming ways to show their love and kindness to others, such as through prayer, speaking kind words, forgiving others, or showing patience with them. Tell kids you'll call out a number from one to four, then kids with that number can hop to be the first to pick up the scrubbie and name a way to show love or kindness. Then everyone will squish their scrubbies as they spell out the way. For example, if "prayer" is named as a way to show kindness, squeeze the scrubbies six times as you call out each letter in the word *prayer*. Continue until all numbers have been called at least twice.

After playing, have kids hug their scrubbies to their cheeks or gently rub them against their faces. Say: **See how your scrubbies are softening? They're not as prickly as before, are they? And the more you play with them, use them, and hug them, the softer and nicer they'll be! You named wonderful ways to show someone love and kindness. Listen to other ways the Bible lists.**

Read aloud Colossians 3:12-14. Then say: **There is such great joy in showing love to others, isn't there? And God's Word teaches us about the joy that comes from sharing love and compassion. Let's begin learning a new Mighty Memory Verse that teaches us about what loving others can do.**

SUPER SCRIPTURE

Before class, write and draw the accompanying arrows for 1 Peter 4:8 on newsprint. (See margin illustration for directions.) Tape the newsprint to the wall or door for kids to see.

Gather kids in front of the Mighty Memory Verse and repeat the verse three times aloud, pointing at the arrows as you repeat the verse. Then say: **The arrows on the verse help us remember the parts. The up arrow stands for the words "above all," which tell us that this verse is very important! The down arrow stands for putting love**

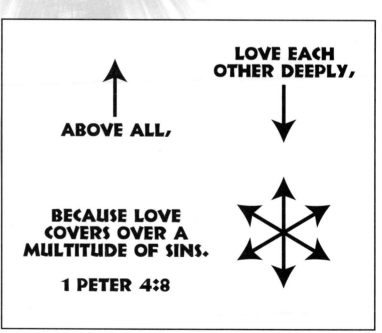

ABOVE ALL,

LOVE EACH OTHER DEEPLY,

BECAUSE LOVE COVERS OVER A MULTITUDE OF SINS.

1 PETER 4:8

down deeply in our hearts for other people. And the multi-directional arrows stand for the ways love covers us—in all directions—and covers the wrong things we say and do. Repeat the verse once more, then ask:

★ **How did Jesus show that love is forgiving when he forgave Zacchaeus?**

★ **Why should we love others even when they do and say wrong things?**

★ **How does loving the hard-to-love make them feel? make us feel? make God feel?**

Say: **Loving others no matter what they do or say is what "unconditional love" means. Jesus loved us unconditionally and even died for us through his love. Loving someone even when they act badly or say unkind things isn't easy, is it? But this is what Jesus calls us to do. And when we show love to someone who is unkind or unlovable, that person can change, just as Zacchaeus did. Love we share from Jesus has amazing power to change lives! We can even change their sad frowns to joyful smiles with our love, so let's change our Unlovey Scrubbies to Smilin' Scrubbies to remind us how love can turn lives around and frowns upside down when we accept and love others!** Have kids gently pull the frowns from their scrubbies and glue them into smiles instead. Then say: **Let's thank Jesus for his amazing, unconditional love that brings us joy and helps us love others.**

Keep the newsprint verse to use next week.

A **POWERFUL** PROMISE

Gather kids in a circle and have them hold their Smilin' Scrubbies. Say: **We've been learning about the joy that comes from loving all people—even the hardest to love. We've discovered that Jesus loves us unconditionally and wants us to love even our enemies. And we've begun to learn a new Mighty Memory Verse that says** (repeat 1 Peter 4:8 with kids), **"Above all, love each other deeply, because love covers over a multitude of sins."**

Hold up the Bible and say: **God's Word teaches us that love can change lives, and we know how Jesus has changed our own lives through his love and forgiveness. Let's pass the Bible around the circle. When you hold the Bible, you can say, "May I love others as Jesus loves me!"** When everyone has had a turn to hold the Bible, end with a corporate "amen."

Say: **Toss your Smilin' Scrubbie across the circle to someone else.** Pause as kids toss their scrubbies. **As you retrieve your Smilin' Scrubbie, give that person a handshake or pat on the shoulder and tell them that they're loved and valued.**

Read aloud 1 Thessalonians 5:16-18a. Then close with this responsive good-bye:

Leader: **May the joy of loving others be with you.**

Children: **And also with you!**

Distribute the Power Page! take-home papers as kids are leaving. Thank children for coming and encourage them to look for ways to be kind and loving to the hardest-to-love people they know this week.

POWER PAGE!

RECIPE FOR L♥VE

Jesus wants us to love others—even our enemies. But it's so hard to know how! Look up 1 Thessalonians 5:15-18, then draw matching lines from the "how" to the correct verse.

Don't pay back wrongs.   verse 16

Be joyful always.   verse 17

Give thanks.   verse 15

Be kind to everyone.   verse 18

Pray constantly.   verse 15

PiCTURE PAL

Let's face it—some people are hard to get along with! But everyone needs love. Make this neat picture frame as a sweet reminder that even the tough-to-love need our prayers!

Whatcha need:

- ♥ plastic picture frame
- ♥ tacky craft glue
- ♥ candy hearts
- ♥ swirled peppermint candies
- ♥ licorice
- ♥ white paper
- ♥ markers

Whatcha do:
Decorate the frame with candies. **Draw** a picture of someone who needs your prayers and friendship. **Slip** the picture in the frame. **Pray** for this person over the next few weeks.

 # LETTER BEFORE

Write the letter that comes before the letter under each space to complete 1 Peter 4:8.

__ __ __ __ __   __ __ __,   __ __ __ __   __ __ __ __   __ __ __ __ __
B C P W F   B M M   M P W F   F B D I   P U I F S

__ __ __ __ __ __,   __ __ __ __ __ __ __   __ __ __ __   __ __ __ __ __
E F F Q M Z   C F D B V T F   M P W F   D P W F S T

__ __ __ __   __   __ __ __ __ __ __ __ __ __   __ __   __ __ __ __ __.
P W F S   B   N V M U J U V E F   P G   T J O T

RESPECT-N-REJOICE!

We honor Jesus when we respect others.

Matthew 8:1-3; 19:13, 14
John 4:7-26
Philippians 2:1-3

SESSION SUPPLIES

★ markers
★ scissors
★ tape
★ construction paper
★ a large plastic bowl
★ clear plastic cups
★ plastic spoons & knives
★ fresh apples, oranges, bananas, & grapes
★ photocopies of the Scripture strip for 1 Peter 4:8 (page 127)
★ photocopies of the Power Page! (page 53)

MIGHTY MEMORY VERSE

Above all, love each other deeply, because love covers over a multitude of sins. 1 Peter 4:8.
(For older kids, add Colossians 3:14: "And over all these virtues put on love, which binds them all together in perfect unity.")

SESSION OBJECTIVES

During this session, children will
★ realize that Jesus came to love and save all people
★ understand what it means to be "inclusive" of people
★ explore ways to show respect to others
★ learn how respecting others honors Jesus and brings everyone joy

BIBLE BACKGROUND

Stop for a moment and think about how much value our society seems to place on exclusivity. Private-issue platinum credit cards, exclusive country-club memberships, private luxury boxes at sports stadiums, and exclusive housing developments or organizations are all designed to fence some people "in" and keep others "out." When we place value on exclusivity, whether consciously or not, we forget that Jesus sought and taught *inclusively* and wants us to do the same. Respect for all people comes through recognizing and valuing differences and seeking to be accepting and inclusive. After all, if

Jesus had formed a club for only the righteous, how desolate and unincluded we would be!

Kids like the feelings of identification and association that accompany "belonging" to special clubs or circles of friends. They likewise understand the unpleasant feelings of being left out, ignored, snubbed, or disrespected. It's important for kids to realize that respecting others involves acceptance, kindness, and love. Use this powerful lesson to help kids discover the joy of respecting others and treating them as we want to be treated.

POWER FOCUS

Before class, cut out 6-inch construction-paper fruits using the patterns in the margin as guides. Cut two fruits for each child. (You'll use one set of paper fruits in this activity and the other set for the Super Scripture activity.)

Warmly welcome kids and let them know you're glad they're in class. Hand each child a paper fruit and have kids form a circle. Say: **We have so many neat things planned for today! We're starting a special club-for-a-day and will be doing some fun activities with delicious fruits. But first we need to make sure everyone belongs in our club. Whoever is standing in the circle at the end of my questions will be in the special club. Are you wearing orange? If so, sit in the center of the circle.** Pause for kids to respond. **Do you have green eyes? If so, sit in the center of the circle.** Pause, then continue. **If you're holding paper apples, sit in the center of the circle. Now does anyone have freckles? If so, sit in the center of the circle.**

By now there should only be a handful of kids left. Ask the next question, then join the kids by sitting in the center of the circle. **Do you have two ears? Then sit in the center of the circle.** Sit with the kids in the center and look quietly around the group. Then say: **It looks like we've excluded everyone from joining the exclusive club, doesn't it?** Ask:

★ **How does it feel when we're excluded from activities or from joining certain groups of people?**

★ How is this the way others feel if they're not included in special activities? in groups of friends? in sports?

★ Did Jesus pick and choose who he would love or forgive? In other words, did Jesus exclude certain people or groups of people from his love? Explain.

Say: **We want to respect and include all people, just as Jesus did. When we exclude people because of their appearance or how they dress, where they live, or if they're guys or girls, we set up walls to keep them away. And not only does that keep joy from growing and spreading, it isn't what Jesus wants us to do. Jesus wants us to respect, love, and include all people so no one feels left out. Let's all stand in a circle to show we *do* belong to a wonderful club—Jesus' club! We're all members of Jesus' club and have a responsibility to respect others as a way to honor and obey Jesus. Today we'll learn about the joy that comes from respecting others and how respecting and accepting others honors Jesus. We'll explore ways to show our respect to others. And we'll review the Mighty Memory Verse we began last week that teaches us the importance of valuing others.** Set the large plastic bowl in the center of the circle. **Place the paper fruits in this bowl, and we'll use them to play a game with the next activity.** Have kids remain standing in a circle.

POWER POINTERS

Read *The Sneeches* by Dr. Seuss to your kids. It's a wonderful illustration of what it means to be exclusive as compared to inclusive and how respecting and including others are powerful ways to encourage peace and joy.

THE **MIGHTY** MESSAGE

Before beginning, draw a heart on two pieces of paper fruit in the bowl. Mix up the fruit pieces, then pass the bowl around the circle and let each child draw out a fruit.

Say: **Let's see how Jesus showed respect for others. I'll give you an example of how Jesus showed respect, then I'll call out "fruit basket upset!" Rush to exchange fruit and places with someone across the circle. The people who end up holding the fruits with hearts on them can answer the questions. Ready?**

Retell the following story from Matthew 8:1-3: **Jesus had just finished teaching a crowd of people when a man with leprosy rushed up to him. Leprosy was a very bad, very contagious skin disease, and most people ran from people with leprosy like they had icky "cooties." When this** man humbly asked Jesus to heal him, Jesus didn't run from the man or try to avoid him. Instead, Jesus touched the man and said, "You are healed"—and he was. Fruit basket upset!

After kids have exchanged places and fruit, ask the following questions and have the kids with hearts on their fruits answer. If they're not sure of the answers, let others volunteer their help. Ask:

★ **How did Jesus show respect for the man with leprosy?**

★ **What if Jesus hadn't wanted to touch the man or help him?**

Say: **Most people wouldn't have wanted that man near them— they'd have thought that he was unclean. But Jesus accepted the man and showed him respect by not running away. Then Jesus demonstrated his love to the man by healing him. Let's see if you can discover how Jesus showed respect in this next story.**

Retell the story of the woman at the well from John 4:7-26: **Jesus came to a well and saw a woman from Samaria. Now most Jews did not like people from Samara and would have nothing to do with Samaritans—especially a woman. But Jesus asked the woman for water, then taught her about the living water he had to offer. Jesus didn't ignore the woman or think she was odd because she was from a foreign country. Instead, Jesus taught her about a time when all God's people, Jews and Samaritans alike, would worship the Lord in spirit and in truth. Fruit basket upset!**

After kids have exchanged places and fruit, ask:

★ **How did Jesus show respect for the Samaritan woman?**

★ **In what ways did Jesus accept the woman and help her?**

Say: **Jesus took the time to speak with someone his friends probably wouldn't have spoken to. Jesus didn't care if the woman was from a dif-**

ferent country, and he didn't care if she was a woman. Jesus showed her respect by accepting and helping her. Wow! You're doing so well. Let's see if you can see how Jesus showed respect in this last example.

Retell the story of how the little children were accepted by Jesus from Matthew 19:13, 14: **Children were brought to Jesus so he could bless them. But Jesus' disciples were angry at the people who bothered**

Jesus. After all, they were just *children*. But Jesus didn't play favorites! Jesus wanted the children to come to him, and he accepted them with open arms. Jesus even said, "Let the children come to me, for the kingdom of heaven belongs to them." Fruit basket upset!

After kids have exchanged places and fruit, ask:

★ **How did Jesus show respect and acceptance for children?**

★ **How was Jesus' respect a demonstration of his love for children?**

Say: **Jesus loved children. Though many people of his time thought kids weren't very important, Jesus knew children are precious, and he respected and accepted them with open arms and a heart full of love!**

Say: **Jesus didn't play favorites. He didn't think one country was better than another or that men were more important than women or adults more valuable than kids. Jesus respected and accepted *all* kinds of people and taught us about respecting others with our hearts and our help. The Bible also teaches us ways to show respect to others. As I read these important ways to show respect, you can write them on your paper fruit.**

Hand each child a marker, then read aloud Galatians 5:22, 23a. After each fruit of the Spirit is read, have kids write it on their paper fruits (for example, "love" or "peace"). Then briefly discuss how each fruit can help us show respect, acceptance, and love to others. Have kids tape their fruits to their shirts or dresses.

Say: **There are so many different people in the world, in our neighborhoods, and at our schools, and Jesus wants us to try to be as respectful and accepting of others as possible. And when we obey Jesus in this way, it brings honor to him and joy to all of us! Let's see how accepting the differences among us can be a cause for real celebration!**

THE MESSAGE IN MOTION

Before class, gather clear plastic cups, plastic spoons and knives, and two each of the following fruits: apples, bananas, bunches of grapes, and oranges. Kids will be preparing fruit parfaits to enjoy. You may also wish to have damp paper towels handy.

Have kids gather around a table, then place the large plastic bowl on the table along with two bananas. Say: **There's nothing as tasty as a fresh, cool fruit salad. Mmmm, fruit is so delicious! But what would be wrong with having only bananas in a fruit salad?** Let kids tell that having only bananas in a fruit salad would be rather boring and give only one kind of taste, texture, and color. Say: **A fruit salad with only one type of fruit isn't really a salad at all. We need lots of different kinds of fruit to make a real fruit salad. Each kind of fruit has its own distinctive color, texture, and taste—and when they're put together, it makes a wonderful mixture of cool, tasty delights!** Ask:

★ **How is respecting lots of people like making a delicious fruit salad?**

★ **In what ways is each person unique, special, and to be respected?**

Say: **It's wonderful when we respect and accept many different people. After all, they all have something to offer, just as each different fruit has something unique to offer a salad. Let's put together our tasty fruit parfaits by adding lots of different fruit to one large bowl.**

Invite kids to form groups that correspond to the paper fruits they're wearing. Have the apples group use plastic knives to cut the apples into slices or chunks, the bananas group to slice bananas into the bowl, the grapes group to pluck grapes into the bowl, and the oranges group to peel and section orange slices into the bowl. When the fruits have been added, mix them gently and let kids spoon the fruits into the clear plastic cups. As kids enjoy their refreshing treats, discuss ways to respect others and talk about how respecting others honors Jesus and brings joy to everyone, including God.

SUPER SCRIPTURE

Before this activity, make sure that 1 Peter 4:8 is still written on the sheet of newsprint and taped to the wall for kids to see. You'll also need to make copies of the Scripture strip for 1 Peter 4:8 from page 127. Cut the strips apart and glue or tape them to the second set of paper fruits you cut earlier. Cut each piece of fruit in half to make mini puzzles. Keep the halves in two separate piles.

Repeat the Mighty Memory Verse three times. (If you have older kids, introduce the extra-challenge verse at this time.) Have kids sit in a circle and distribute one half of the paper-fruit halves. Explain that in this activity you'll begin passing other halves of fruit around the circle. As soon as someone makes a match with his piece of fruit, he is to jump up, and all passing will stop. The child can repeat the verse, then sit back in the circle, and the passing will begin again. Continue until all the pieces of fruit have been matched and each child has a copy of the Mighty Memory Verse on a paper fruit. Then ask:

★ **How does showing respect for others also show our love?**

★ **Can there be love without respect? Explain.**

Say: **Jesus wants us to respect, accept, and love others because he knows that there is joy in being kind to people. When we respect others and treat them the way we want to be treated, it shows our love and acceptance—and it honors Jesus in a wonderful way!**

Let's honor Jesus in another wonderful way through a powerful prayer from Scripture. Keep the newsprint verse to use next week.

A POWERFUL PROMISE

Have kids sit in a group. Say: **We've been exploring what it means to respect others and how respecting people honors Jesus and brings joy to everyone. We've discovered ways that Jesus respected and accepted people. And we've reviewed our Mighty Memory Verse that says** (lead kids in repeating 1 Peter 4:8 with you), **"Above all, love each other deeply, because love covers over a multitude of sins."** (Repeat the extra-challenge verse, if you're learning it.)

Say: **Remember when we began our time together and we were excluded from the special group? We sat in a group like we are now. Let's see if we can reverse the process and be included in the special group who loves Jesus.**

Read the following prayer based on Philippians 2:1-3 as you form a standing circle: **If you have any encouragement from being together with Jesus, stand up and join the circle. If you have any comfort from Jesus' love, join the circle. If you have any fellowship with the Spirit or feel tenderness and compassion, then join the circle.** Everyone should now be standing in a circle. Join hands and continue: **Now make my joy complete by being like-minded, having the same love, being one in spirit and purpose. Do nothing out of selfish ambition or vain conceit, but in humility consider others better than yourselves. Amen.**

If there's time, sing the Joy Song from page 17, then end with this responsive good-bye:

Leader: **May you respect others as Jesus respects us.**

Children: **And also you!**

Distribute the Power Page! take-home papers as kids are leaving. Thank children for coming and encourage them to look for ways to respect, accept, and love others in the coming week.

POWER PAGE!

GREATEST COMMAND

Complete the puzzle and fill in the missing words at the bottom to discover what Jesus commands us.

opposite of under ___ ___ ___ ___
                     1   2   3   4

a little cool ___ ___ ___ ___ ___ ___
               5   6   7   8   8   9

opposite of happy ___ ___ ___
                   10 11 12

snip with scissors ___ ___ ___
                     5 13 14

___ ___ ___ ___ ___ ___ ___ ___ ___ ___ ___ ___
 8 1 2 3   3 11 5 6   1 14 6 3 4

___ ___ ___ ___ ___ ___ ___
11 10 7 6 11 2 3

___ ___ ___ ___ ___ ___ ___ ___ .
 8 1 2 3 12 9 1 13

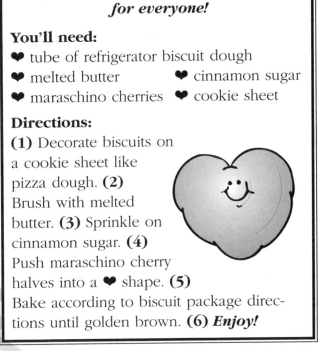

ONE FOR ALL!

Make this yummy bread and share the treat with everyone in your family as you remind them that Jesus' love is for everyone!

You'll need:
- ♥ tube of refrigerator biscuit dough
- ♥ melted butter
- ♥ cinnamon sugar
- ♥ maraschino cherries
- ♥ cookie sheet

Directions:
(1) Decorate biscuits on a cookie sheet like pizza dough. **(2)** Brush with melted butter. **(3)** Sprinkle on cinnamon sugar. **(4)** Push maraschino cherry halves into a ♥ shape. **(5)** Bake according to biscuit package directions until golden brown. **(6)** *Enjoy!*

Crazy Circuit Board

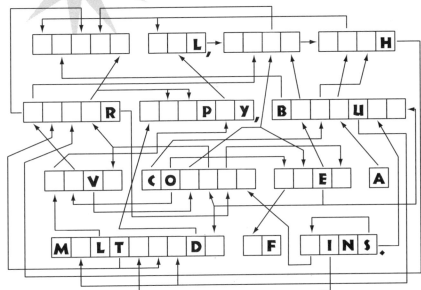

Follow the arrows to plug in the missing letters from 1 Peter 4:8.

JOY CHANGES

We can rejoice through the changes Jesus' death and resurrection bring!

John 16:20, 22
Hebrews 12:2
Peter 1:8, 9

SESSION SUPPLIES

★ Bibles
★ construction paper
★ scissors
★ 1-inch-wide ribbon
★ black socks
★ tacky craft glue
★ black craft felt
★ photocopies of the devotion directions box (page 58)
★ photocopies of the Whiz Quiz (page 62) and the Power Page! (page 61)

MIGHTY MEMORY VERSE

Above all, love each other deeply, because love covers over a multitude of sins. 1 Peter 4:8.

(For older kids, add Colossians 3:14: "And over all these virtues put on love, which binds them all together in perfect unity.")

SESSION OBJECTIVES

During this session, children will
★ understand Jesus' joy in dying for us
★ discover how sadness can turn to joy
★ learn that joy through Jesus' sacrifice never fades away
★ express thanks for Jesus' joyous sacrifice of love

BIBLE BACKGROUND

Sacrifice and *joy* are perhaps two of the most unlikely-to-be-related words, especially in our world today. The attitudes of the "me" generation and a desire not to "get involved" keep us from associating two words that seem to have such opposite meanings. Yet Jesus pulled sacrifice and joy powerfully together on the cross in the greatest act of love, sacrifice, and obedience the world will ever know. Hebrews 12:2 tells us of the joy with which Jesus endured the cross and the love he freely gave to us through the sacrifice of his life in exchange for our sins. How amazing that one of Jesus' last feelings this side of heaven, even as he endured the cross, was one of joy!

Though most kids are ready and willing to help others, share toys, and give away outgrown clothes with ease, it's much more difficult for them to sacrifice something of great personal price—let alone receive *joy* from that sacrifice. But if kids are fully to understand what Jesus did for us on the cross, they need to realize that Jesus willingly died for our sins and, more surprisingly, sacrificed his life for us with *joy!* Use this thoughtful lesson to help kids realize the pain-transcending joy Jesus felt in his ultimate act of love for us.

POWER FOCUS

Before class, collect bright 1-inch-wide ribbon; pairs of clean, black socks (children's or adults—one sock for each child, plus one extra); black craft felt; and tacky craft glue. Kids will be making their own Joy-Changers later in the lesson, but you'll want to make one for this activity. To make a Joy Changer, simply cut a 2-by-3-inch black-felt rectangle and glue it inside the ankle of a black sock to make a secret pocket. Be sure the short edge of the rectangle is even with the edge of the sock's ankle. While the sock dries, cut a 2-foot length of bright ribbon and roll it into a small ball to fit inside the secret pocket of the sock.

↓ Open edge

Before the activity, slip the ribbon inside the secret pocket and carefully hold the pocket closed. When it's time to reveal the ribbon, simply pull it out of the pocket. You'll also need to cut a 2-foot length of ribbon for each child.

Warmly welcome kids and tell them you're happy they've come. Invite kids to tell about things that make them sad or disappointed, such as a family member's illness, a friend moving away, or a pet who might be lost.

Hold up the black sock, being careful to hold the secret pocket closed. Say: **Sadness, grief, and disappointment can often feel like this black sock—dark and empty.** Turn the sock inside out, again being careful to seal the pocket. Show kids the empty inside of the sock as you continue: **Sadness makes us feel as though there's no joy in our hearts, and it can really turn us inside out.** Turn the sock right side out. **But Jesus wants us to know that the joy he puts in our hearts is joy that is always there no**

matter what. And it's joy that can turn sadness into celebration! Quickly pull out the ribbon and wave it around as you slyly set the sock aside.

Say: **The Bible even tells us that "weeping may remain for a night, but rejoicing comes in the morning"** (Psalm 30:5b). **That means that grief and sadness can amazingly turn to joy—especially when we know what precious gifts Jesus has given us. Today we'll discover how sadness and grief can turn to joy even when things seem empty and black. We'll explore how Jesus' love and forgiveness bring us joy that lasts forever. And we'll learn that Jesus felt joy in sacrificing his life for us on the cross. These ribbons will help us as we learn some amazing truths about Jesus and his everlasting joy.** Hand each child a ribbon.

THE **MIGHTY** MESSAGE

Have kids scatter around the room and hold their ribbons. Say: **One of the saddest times in all the world was when Jesus died for our sins. Jesus' disciples didn't quite understand what was going on, and they thought their beloved Lord was gone after he suffered on the cross. Let's use our ribbons to act out the story of Jesus' greatest act of love and see if we can understand how such deep sadness turned to jubilant joy!**

Jesus had spent his life loving and teaching others and obeying God. (Sweep the ribbons back and forth.) **And though many people loved Jesus in return, some didn't. These people refused to listen to the truth and wanted to hurt Jesus.** (Snap the ribbons up and down.) **Jesus was whipped and hung on a cross that was tall** (hold the ribbons vertically) **and wide** (hold the ribbons horizontally).

Quietly continue: **Jesus died for our sins. He died because he wanted us to be close to God, and this was the only way to accomplish that. Jesus willingly sacrificed his life for us because he loved us.** (Slowly wrap the ribbons around you.) Read aloud Hebrews 12:2. Then say: **Jesus willingly and with** *joy* **gave his life for us. The disciples were very sad and confused. They didn't understand why Jesus had to die, and they thought they would never see him or be happy again.**

POWER POINTERS

List requests for forgiveness and "give" these requests to Jesus through prayer. Then toss away the papers to show that Jesus removes the barriers to joy through his forgiveness.

For three days Jesus was in the tomb—one, two, three. (Swoop three big circles using the ribbons.) **But on the third day, when Mary and her friends went to the tomb, their grief turned to joy!** (Joyously wave the ribbons.) **Jesus was risen, and those who loved him knew then the love Jesus had given them! And they remembered what Jesus had told them.** (Read aloud John 16:20b and 22.) **Jesus had promised that their sadness would be turned to joy and that no one could ever take that joy away from them. Yeah!** (Cheer using the ribbons.) **Jesus gave us his love, his forgiveness, eternal life, and the promise of eternal joy!**

Have kids sit in place, then ask:

★ **Why did Jesus give his life for us?**

★ **In what ways does Jesus' sacrifice bring joy?**

★ **How could Jesus have felt joy at giving up his life for us?**

★ **Why can this powerful joy never be taken away from us?**

Say: **Jesus gave us so many gifts when he gave up his own life for us. He gave us love, forgiveness, eternal life, a chance to be friends with God again, and amazing joy! Jesus knew we would have times of grief and sadness, but he also knew the joy he sets before us will always be with us. As long as we love Jesus and accept his forgiveness into our lives, we have the joy and hope of eternal life with him!** Read aloud 1 Peter 1:8, 9. Ask:

★ **How does it give us joy to know we have the promise of eternal life?**

★ **How can Jesus' joy make even the toughest times seem easier and brighter?**

Say: **Even when times seem dark, empty, and hopeless, we have joy from Jesus to get us through. Isn't that an awesome truth? Jesus was right when he said, "You will grieve, but your grief will turn to joy"** (John 16:20b). **Let's make Joy-Changers so you can pass the joy to someone else by reminding them that Jesus' joy lasts a lifetime and beyond!**

THE MESSAGE IN **MOTION**

Before class, be sure you have a black sock for each child. Kids will be making Joy-Changers like the one you used in the Power Focus activity. You'll also need black craft felt, scissors, and tacky craft glue.

Let kids work in pairs or trios to make their Joy-Changers. Have kids cut small felt rectangles to glue to the inside edges of the socks to make the secret pockets. As the felt rectangles dry, lead kids in singing the Joy Song to the tune of Old MacDonald. Use your colorful ribbons to wave joyously as you sing.

JOY SONG

There is joy down in my heart, (point to your heart)
And Jesus put it there! (point upward)
Joy that cannot fade away (shake your finger "no")
And follows everywhere! (turn around in place)
J-O-Y, sign it high— (sign the letters for "joy" two times)
Jump for joy and give high fives! (jump, then give high fives)
There is joy down in my heart, (point to your heart)
And Jesus put it there! (point upward)

J
O
Y

After singing, have kids fold up their ribbons and slip them in the secret sock pockets. Hand out copies of the devotion box below, then lead kids in practicing the devotion using their Joy-Changers.

WHAT TO SAY:	**WHAT TO DO:**
★ We all have times when we feel sad or disappointed.	*Hold sock up and show both sides.*
★ Sadness and grief can make us feel empty and turned inside out.	*Turn the sock inside out, carefully holding the pocket closed.*
★ But Jesus promises that our grief will turn to joy …	*Pull out the ribbon and wave it around.*
★ and nothing will take our joy away!	*Hold the ribbon securely in both hands.*
"You will grieve, but your grief will turn to joy." John 16:20	

After kids have practiced the devotion, challenge them to present this mini devotion to three people during the coming week to remind them where their joy comes from and how Jesus' joy can never be taken away. Then say: **We receive so much joy from Jesus' words, don't we? There's joy in all of**

God's Word! Let's review our Mighty Memory Verse and see how Jesus' death and joyous resurrection brings us even more joy.

SUPER SCRIPTURE

Be sure you still have 1 Peter 4:8 written on newsprint and taped to the wall. Cut a construction-paper heart large enough to cover a few words or portions of words of the verse at one time.

Gather kids by the newsprint and repeat the verse two times in unison. (If you're learning the extra-challenge verse, review it at this time and use the paper heart to cover portions of this verse too.) Then hand the heart to a child and invite her to cover up several words and call on another child to repeat the entire verse, including the hidden portion. If the verse is repeated correctly, that child may then hide words and call on someone to repeat the verse. Continue until all kids have had a turn to cover words and repeat the verse at least once.

Say: **What a very important verse this is! It speaks of love and how it covers a multitude of sins. Think of the story of Jesus dying for our sins.** Ask:

★ **How did love fit into Jesus' death on the cross?**
★ **In what ways did Jesus' love offer us forgiveness and cover a multitude of our sins?**
★ **Why do you think it brings us joy when we love others? when we forgive others?**

Say: **Jesus was the only one who could forgive our sins and make peace between God and us. But we can do our part to forgive other people of the wrong and hurtful things they say and do. And we can ask forgiveness when we act in unkind ways. Jesus willingly died to forgive our sins, and he did this with joy and perfect love. As 1 Peter 4:8 reminds us, when we love others and are forgiving, it brings peace, love, and joy to ourselves, others, and Jesus! Let's close with a prayer thanking Jesus for his sacrifice of love that brings us everlasting life, love, and joy.**

A POWERFUL PROMISE

Have kids sit in a circle and hold their Joy-Changers. Say: **What a good time we've been having learning about the joy that came from such a**

sad event as Jesus' death. We've discovered that Jesus' death was the saddest time of all but that it led to the greatest joy of all. We've learned that joy from Jesus can never be taken away, and we've explored how Jesus felt joy when he willingly sacrificed his life to forgive our sins. Our Mighty Memory Verse teaches us about love covering a multitude of sins too. As 1 Peter 4:8 says (lead kids in repeating the Mighty Memory Verse with you), "Above all, love each other deeply, because love covers over a multitude of sins."

(Repeat the extra-challenge verse, if kids have been learning it.)

Say: Let's use our Joy-Changers to offer a prayer to Jesus and thank him for the joy we find in his sacrifice of love. Follow along with your Joy-Changers as we pray.

Dear Lord, once we lived in a sad, dark world. (Hold up the socks.)

Our hearts were empty, and no joy was around us. (Turn the socks inside out.)

But through your death and resurrection, we have found perfect love and joy! (Pull out the ribbons and wave them in the air.)

Thank you for willingly and joyfully giving up your life so we could be forgiven. Thank you for the joy you give that can never be taken away. Amen. (Wave the ribbons, then hold them to your hearts.)

Before kids leave, allow five or ten minutes to complete the Whiz Quiz from page 62. If you run out of time, be sure to do this page first thing next week. The Whiz Quiz is an invaluable tool that allows kids, teachers, and parents see what kids have learned in the previous three weeks.

Read aloud Romans 4:7, then end with this responsive good-bye:

Leader: **May Jesus' love and joy be with you.**

Children: **And also with you!**

Distribute the Power Page! take-home papers as kids are leaving. Thank children for coming and encourage them to present their mini devotion to three people this week.

POWER PAGE!

JOY-A-COMIN'!

Read John 16:22, then use the key to fill in the words to the joyous promise Jesus made to us.

A	D	E	G	I	J	K	L
☆	♣	➌	✓	✳	✖	✧	✎

N	O	R	S	T	U	W	Y
◆	●	✮	■	✝	♥	✺	❤

___ ___ ___ ___ ___ ___ ___ ___ ___ ___ ___

___ ___ ___ ___ ___ ___ ___ ___ ___ ___ ___

___ ___ ___ ___ ___ ___ ___ ___ ___ ___ ___

___ ___ ___ ___ ___ ___ ___ ___ ___ ___ ___

Change Game

Want some family fun? Cut out six squares, then cut the squares into 12 triangles. See if you can change and rearrange the ▲s to make the following shapes:

- ▲ a flower
- ▲ a house
- ▲ a butterfly
- ▲ a heart
- ▲ a star
- ▲ a cross

As you play, have family members name ways we are changed through Jesus' love and forgiveness.

Seek-n-Search

Find the words to 1 Peter 4:8 in the grid, then write them in the spaces.

___ ___ ___ ___ ___ ___ ___ , ___ ___ ___ ___

___ ___ ___ ___ ___ ___

___ ___ ___ ___ ___ , ___ ___ ___ ___

___ ___ ___ ___ ___ ___ ___ ___ ___ ___

___ ___ ___ ___ ___ ___ ___ ___ ___ ___ .

Q	M	B	E	C	A	U	S	E
M	U	L	T	I	T	U	D	E
W	C	O	V	E	R	S	X	O
I	O	V	E	R	L	L	O	T
D	E	E	P	L	Y	O	F	H
A	A	N	A	B	O	V	E	E
H	C	T	L	O	V	E	Z	R
O	H	Y	L	S	I	N	S	R

WHIZ QUIZ

Color in Yes or No to answer the questions.

✓ Jesus wants us to be mean to our enemies. (YES) (NO)

✓ It's not always easy to love everyone. (YES) (NO)

✓ Jesus wants us to include others. (YES) (NO)

✓ When we respect others, we honor Jesus. (YES) (NO)

✓ Joy comes from Jesus' forgiveness. (YES) (NO)

✓ Our joy can be taken away. (YES) (NO)

⊙ Scripture Swirl ⊙

Write the words to 1 Peter 4:8, the
MIGHTY MEMORY VERSE,
around the swirl. Use the words in
the box below, if needed.

Above

other	because
love	over
sins	love
all	covers
a	deeply
each	of
multitude	

JOY THROUGH JESUS' PROMISES

May your unfailing love come
to me, O LORD, your salvation
according to your promise.
Psalm 119:41

THE JOYFUL WAY!

Jesus promises us the true way to God.

Psalm 90:14
John 14:6, 12
1 Corinthians 8:6
1 Peter 1:8

SESSION SUPPLIES

★ Bibles
★ masking & clear tape
★ markers & scissors
★ dowel rods & glitter glue
★ plastic cups
★ white poster board
★ modeling dough
★ photocopies of John 14:6 (page 68)
★ photocopies of the Scripture strip for Psalm 119:41 (page 127)
★ photocopies of the Power Page! (page 71)

MIGHTY MEMORY VERSE

May your unfailing love come to me, O LORD, your salvation according to your promise. Psalm 119:41.

SESSION OBJECTIVES

During this session, children will
★ discover there's only one way to God
★ learn that Jesus is the way, truth, and life
★ realize there's joy in making Jesus our leader
★ explore how faith helps us joyfully follow Jesus

BIBLE BACKGROUND

Think for a moment about different *crossroads* you may have come to in your life, times and situations in which the decisions you made had great or grave consequences. Was it a crossroads of relationships or perhaps one focused on employment or educational choices? Often critical and always confusing, crossroads by their very nature point us in different directions and demand a choice of paths. Isn't it wonderful that when it comes to finding our way to God, Jesus makes it very clear that he is the only path to choose? In John 14:6, Jesus succinctly states that he alone is the way, the truth, and the life that leads to our heavenly Father. Next time you come to a crossroads, consider the "cross" in crossroads and turn to face the only direction that provides heavenly guidance—toward Jesus!

Kids are just beginning to discover that their choices do have consequences. Taking that forbidden before-dinner cookie could lead to: (a) early bedtime; (b) a stern "talking to"; (c) no desserts for a week; or (d) all of the above. But cookies crumble when compared to the choice of paths life presents to kids even in their early years. It's important for kids to realize that there's only way to God: through Jesus. Use this lesson to help kids discover that joy comes from choosing to travel with Jesus along his heavenly pathway to God.

POWER FOCUS

Before class, arrange chairs around the room to make an obstacle course. At one end of the room, tape a "Go" sign on the wall, then tape a "Stop" sign on the opposite wall. Kids will be traveling through the obstacle course from the go sign to the stop sign in various ways.

Warmly welcome kids and let them know you're glad they're present. Explain that you'll begin your time by a different kind of follow-the-leader game. Form three lines by the go sign. Designate the first players in each line as leaders. Explain that in this activity, the leaders will lead their groups around the obstacle course to the stop sign. Leaders may choose any paths they'd like and may skip, tiptoe, walk backwards, or travel in any ways they choose while the followers imitate the actions. When the stop sign is reached, have new leaders lead groups back to the starting place. Continue until everyone has had a chance to be the leader.

When you're done, ask:

★ **What responsibilities does a good leader have?**

★ **What responsibilities do good followers have?**

★ **How did you choose which path you wanted to take to reach the stop sign?**

★ **In what ways is this game like choosing the right way to God?**

Say: **In our game there were many paths that led to the goal, and all those ways were fun to travel. But in life, there's only one way to reach God, and we must follow that way carefully. Today we'll discover what the true way to God is and how we can follow the right path to reach our goal. We'll explore how faith helps us be good followers, and we'll also begin learning a new Mighty Memory Verse that teaches us about joy through heavenly promises. Right now, let's use some familiar road signs to help us discover the way to God.**

THE **MIGHTY** MESSAGE

Before this activity, make four poster-board road signs using the margin illustrations as guides. Make each sign about as large as a paper plate.

Form a large standing circle and have kids number off by fours. Have kids identify the signs and the words on them, then place the road sings in the center. Say: **Perhaps the most important truth we'll ever learn is the truth about the true way to find God. Listen carefully as I read some important Scripture verses. Then I'll call out a number and the players with that number can hop to pick up the road sign they feel symbolizes what I've just read.**

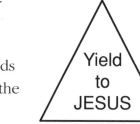

Read the following verses, breaking them into parts. If kids choose a sign different from the one suggested, have them explain their choices.

★ *John 14:6a:* **"Jesus answered, 'I am the way and the truth and the life.'"** (One Way sign)

★ *John 14:6b:* **"No one comes to the Father except through me."** (Stop sign)

★ *John 14:12:* **"I tell you the truth, anyone who has faith in me will do what I have been doing. He will do even greater things than these, because I am going to the Father."** (Go sign)

★ *1 Corinthians 8:6:* **"Yet for us there is but one God, the Father, from whom all things came and for whom we live; and there is but one Lord, Jesus Christ, through whom all things came and through whom we live."** (One Way sign)

★ *1 Peter 1:8:* **"Though you have not seen him, you love him; and even though you do not see him now, you believe in him and are filled with an inexpressible and glorious joy."** (Yield to Jesus sign)

POWER POINTERS

It would be great if someone can make block-type stands for the One Way signs kids will make! Cut the blocks from 2-by-4s and drill a hole to fit a thick dowel rod in the center of each block.

Say: **You did very well in choosing the signs! I think the most important sign of all is the One Way sign, because it reminds us that there's only one way to God: through Jesus! Jesus promised us that the one true way to God is through him and through following him.** Ask:

★ **How does making Jesus our leader help us find God?**

★ **What can we do to be good followers of Jesus so we'll stay on the right path to God?**

★ **In what ways does faith help us follow Jesus?**

Say: **There's such joy in making Jesus the leader of our lives! Just think: you wouldn't want to follow someone who didn't know the way to our goal or took dangerous paths, would you? We want the one leader, the one Lord, who can lead us to God, who is our goal. Jesus knows the way, and it's only through loving, obeying, and accepting Jesus into our lives that we will find life with God. That's why Jesus said he is the way and the truth and the life! Let's make cool One Way signs as giant reminders of the one true way to find joy and our Father in heaven.**

THE MESSAGE IN MOTION

Before class, collect a plastic cup, a sheet of white poster board, and a thin 3-foot dowel rod for each child. Cut out several large One Way arrow patterns for kids to trace and cut out. This large-as-life craft will impress your kids, and they'll love setting it around their homes as powerful reminders of Jesus' promise to show them the one way to God. You'll also need markers, glitter glue, modeling dough, scissors, tape, and copies of the Scripture box for John 14:6 from this activity. (If you have someone to make wooden stands with holes, you can delete the cups and modeling dough. See the Power Pointer.)

Invite kids to work in pairs or trios and explain they'll be making large, stand-up One Way signs to set around their rooms and homes. Have kids each trace

67

and cut out two large arrows using the patterns you provide. Tape a dowel rod securely to the center of one arrow, then tape or staple the other arrow, sandwich style, over the dowel rod to make a two-sided sign. Write "ONE WAY" in thick letters across both arrows. Glue the verse box for John 14:6 below the letters. Glitter glue the edges of the arrows.

Finally, stuff plastic cups half full with modeling dough to weight the cups. Poke the dowel rods down through the dough. (Caution kids to lift their signs using the cups and not the rods, since the rods will pull out of the dough until it hardens!)

When kids are done making their signs, say: **Set your One Way sign around your home to remind everyone in your family that the one true way to joy, eternal life, and God is through Jesus. God's Word teaches us about finding our way to God. And it also teaches us about the joy-filled promises Jesus gives us. Let's discover one of those promises with a new Mighty Memory Verse.**

> **JESUS ANSWERED, "I AM THE WAY AND THE TRUTH AND THE LIFE. NO ONE COMES TO THE FATHER EXCEPT THROUGH ME." (JOHN 14:6)**

SUPER SCRIPTURE

Before class, enlarge and redraw the Scripture picture from the margin. Be sure to add the words "love" and "salvation." Then write the words to Psalm 119:41 below the picture. Tape the picture to the wall or a door for kids to see. You'll also need copies of the Scripture strip for Psalm 119:41 from page 127, one for each child.

Gather kids by the Scripture picture. Point to the picture as you repeat the words to the verse as

follows: **May your unfailing love come to me, O LORD** (point to the word *love,* to the figure, then to the cloud), **your salvation according to your promise** (point to the word *salvation*).

Say: **This wonderful verse teaches us that we're promised two joy-filled things from the Lord—his love and salvation. Wow! What joy givers! And the best thing about the Lord's promises is that he keeps them. Promises from God and from Jesus are promises we can count on, promises that bring us hope and joy in even the darkest of times. We've been learning that Jesus promised us one way to God: through him. Our Mighty Memory Verse tells us two other promises that bring joy.** Ask:

★ **Why does trusting the Lord's promises bring us joy?**

★ **How does faith help us wait for the Lord's promises to be kept?**

Hand out the Scripture strips for Psalm 119:41 and have kids glue the verses to their One Way signs and read them aloud. Then say: **Our Mighty Memory Verse comes from the book of Psalms in the Bible. The book of Psalms is filled with poems or psalms that are full of hope, celebration, and joy. Listen to another wonderful verse from Psalm 90 and see if you can hear the word *joy* in the verse. When you do, turn to someone and give a high five.**

Read aloud Psalm 90:14 and wait for kids to give their high fives. Then say: **God's Word teaches us about what joy is, about where we find joy, and about how joy makes us feel. Psalm 90:14 asks us to express our joy through singing, so let's sing our Joy Song!**

Lead children in singing and doing the actions to the Joy Song from page 17 to the tune of Old MacDonald. After singing, say: **Can you feel the joy in your hearts? Joy can turn the darkest times into the brightest hopes as we wait for God's promises to be fulfilled. Let's offer a prayer of thanks for the Lord's love and promises that bring us such wonderful joy!**

A **POWERFUL** PROMISE

Gather kids in a circle and say: **We've had fun today learning that there's only one way to God: through Jesus and his promises. We've discovered that making Jesus our one leader keeps us on the right path to God. And we've begun learning a new Mighty Memory Verse that says** (lead kids in repeating Psalm 119:41), **"May your unfailing love come to me, O LORD, your salvation according to your promise."**

Hold up the Bible and say: **God promises us many things in the Bible. He promises to be with us, to love us, to offer us salvation, and to show us the way to heaven. He also promises us unfailing joy when we follow Jesus. Let's promise to make Jesus our leader and stay on the right path to our heavenly Father. We'll pass the Bible around the circle. When it's your turn to hold the Bible, you can say, "I want Jesus to be the leader of my life."** Continue until everyone has had a turn to hold the Bible, then end with a corporate "amen."

Say: **Jesus tells us he is the way and the truth and the life. And he promises that if we follow him, our joy will never end. When you go home today, place your One Way sign in a place where everyone in your family can be reminded that there's only one way to truth, one way to life, and one way to joy!**

Read aloud Acts 2:28, then close with this responsive good-bye:

Leader: **May the joy of Jesus and his promises be with you.**

Children: **And also with you!**

Distribute the Power Page! take-home papers as kids are leaving. Thank children for coming and encourage them to keep their promises to make Jesus the leader of their lives this week and always. Suggest that kids use their One Way signs to remind them of their commitments.

POWER PAGE!

ONE WAY

A-MAZE-ING

Follow the maze to find how we get to God.

Fill in the missing words to John 14:6. Then decode the sentence below to discover where Jesus points us.

_ _ _ _ _ _ _ _ _ _ _ ,
4   12   1   7   5

" _ _ _ the _ _ _ and the
         10 11

_ _ _ _ _ and the _ _ _ _ .
    3   2

No _ _ _ comes to the
    9 13

_ _ _ _ _ except
      6

_ _ _ _ _ _ me."
8   14

_ _ _ _ _ _ _ _ _ _
4 7 1 3 1   2 1 6 8 7

_ _ _ _ _ _ _ _ _ _ _ !
9 13 7 10 12 11 6 9 14 9 5

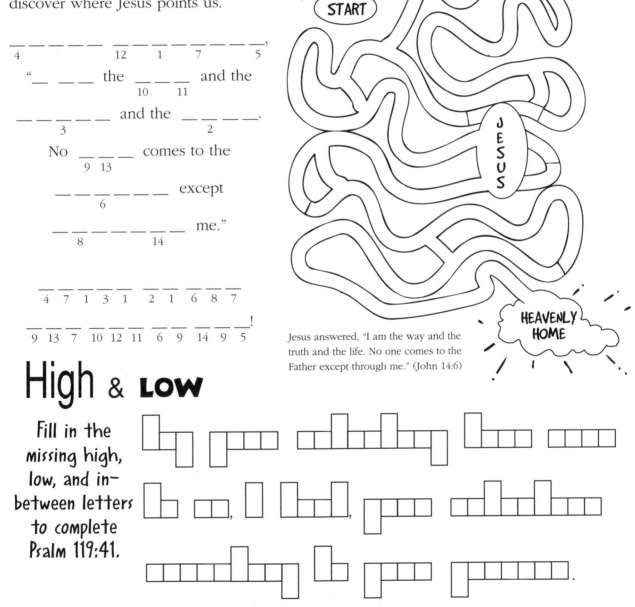

Jesus answered, "I am the way and the truth and the life. No one comes to the Father except through me." (John 14:6)

High & LOW

Fill in the missing high, low, and in-between letters to complete Psalm 119:41.

SAVED FOR JOY

Our joy is great when we've been saved by Christ!

Luke 15:3-7; Titus 3:5;
2 Corinthians 4:8; Luke 10:20

SESSION SUPPLIES

- ★ Bibles
- ★ lemonade, cups
- ★ pans of water & mud
- ★ plaster of Paris
- ★ cotton balls, felt
- ★ markers, glue
- ★ newspaper, gravel
- ★ Styrofoam packing peanuts
- ★ powdered bubble bath
- ★ candy confetti or sprinkles
- ★ stapler, tape
- ★ self-sealing sandwich bags
- ★ photocopies of the Scripture strip for Psalm 119:41 (page 127)
- ★ photocopies of the Power Page! (page 79)

MIGHTY MEMORY VERSE

May your unfailing love come to me, O Lord, your salvation according to your promise. Psalm 119:41.
(For older kids, add in John 14:6: "I am the way and the truth and the life. No one comes to the Father except through me.")

SESSION OBJECTIVES

During this session, children will
- ★ discover how salvation brings us joy
- ★ learn that our salvation brings joy to God
- ★ realize that Jesus wants us to have joy in our salvation

BIBLE BACKGROUND

Few things can bring God as much joy as when his children choose to embrace Jesus with their lives. By accepting the gift of salvation Jesus has set before us and by professing our choice lovingly, we find inexpressible and glorious joy! Perhaps no other verses sum it up as beautifully as 1 Peter 1:8, 9: "Though you have not seen him, you love him; and even though you do not see him now, you believe in him and are filled with an inexpressible and glorious joy, for you are receiving the goal of your faith, the salvation of your souls."

Ever had a child of your own or one in class throw a tantrum out of anger or frustration? How about a child impulsively throwing her arms around your neck in a big bear hug? Most kids express their feelings with honesty, abandonment, and passion. Their budding joy at knowing, loving, and following Jesus yearns for expression, though most kids may be unsure of how to show this new-found joy. Use this joy-filled lesson to help kids realize the many ways they can express their love and joy for Jesus and the joyous promise of salvation he offers us.

POWER FOCUS

Before class, prepare a pitcher of cool, refreshing lemonade. Provide a clear, plastic cup for each child. Fill several pans with water; fill another pan with mud. You may wish to spread newspapers or a plastic paint drop cloth under the pans to protect the floor. Place the pans on the floor covering. Place the pitcher of lemonade in plain view.

Warmly welcome the kids and give each one a plastic cup. As you pass out the cups, tell the kids that you have a refreshing drink for them and show them the pitcher of lemonade.

Say: **Before we have our drink, we need to prepare our cups.** Ask the kids to dip their cups in the pan of mud. Then ask who wants to use their cups to taste the lemonade. Start to pour the lemonade into the kids' dirty cups. Allow the kids to refuse the drink. Say: **Why don't you want some of this lemonade? It's cool and refreshing and quite tasty. What's wrong with it?** Allow kids to talk about the dirt in their cups.

These dirty cups are similar to a person's life with sin in it—dirty and not very useable. How can we make these cups useable again? Right, by cleaning them. Have the kids clean their cups in a pan of water, then pour lemonade for each child. **How does that taste? Much better than it would have with the dirt, right? That's the way it is when God saves us. He makes us clean by washing away our sins. Then we can be filled with his joy, love, and truth. God's Holy Spirit lives in us, and we can do wonderful things with God living in us. What a gift! What joy that brings!**

Today we'll discover how being saved brings us joy and pleases God. We'll explore what it means to be saved and review the Mighty Memory Verse we've been learning that teaches us about the joy we have in Jesus' promises of love and salvation.

Right now, let's learn more about the joy that God feels when one person is saved.

THE MIGHTY MESSAGE

Before class, prepare a plaster paperweight for each student. Provide enough plaster of Paris to make 9 ounces for each child. Use 9-ounce clear plastic cups (ones that are shorter and wider than most cups). Prepare the plaster as directed on the package and completely fill one cup for each child. Collect cotton balls, felt for lamb ears, glue, and permanent markers to decorate the cups of plaster. Also, gather a few sheets of newspaper, a cup-full of Styrofoam packing peanuts, and a cup-full of gravel or small stones.

Gather the kids around a table with the paperweight supplies. Give each child a cotton ball. Say: **Jesus told stories, called parables, to help people understand about God. Many of the Jewish leaders could not understand why Jesus spent time with sinners. But Jesus knew that people who had sin in their lives needed God, and they needed to repent. To *repent* means to be sorry for the wrong things we've done and to change our ways so we don't repeat those sins.**

The story we're going to read is about a shepherd who had 100 sheep. While you listen to the story, pretend the cotton ball you are holding is a sheep.

Invite volunteers to read aloud Luke 15:3-6. Then talk about how important one person is to God. Ask:

★ **How many sheep did the man lose?**

★ **How important was that one sheep to the shepherd?**

★ **What did the man do when he found the lost sheep?**

Say: **Each of us is like that one sheep. We are very important to God and he wants us to be saved.** Read Luke 15:7. **Just like the shepherd who celebrated with his friends, all of heaven rejoices when one person repents and is saved! The salvation of just one person brings joy to God!**

Being saved also brings us joy. Remember when you had the dirty cup? Even though you had the promise of getting a drink, you weren't happy because dirt and lemonade just don't go together! Only after you had cleaned your cup were you able to enjoy the lemonade that I promised. It's the same way with God's promise for salvation. Have a volun-

POWER POINTERS

This is an excellent time to invite a children's minister or other church leader in to visit about being saved and what it means.

teer read Titus 3:5. **You see, just like we washed the dirt from our cups so that we could receive the lemonade, God saves us through the washing away of our sins through Jesus.**

And that's not the only reason why we should be joyful about our salvation.

★ **How many of you have ever gotten into trouble and then promised not to do it again?**

★ **How many of you then did it again anyhow? Even though we washed our cups earlier, we could still dip them back into the mud.**

★ **How do we keep ourselves from getting dirty again?** Allow students to respond.

Give each child a clean plastic cup. Take a handful of packing peanuts. **The best way to keep the dirt out of a cup is to put something else inside. It's the same with our lives. When God washes away our sins, he gives us a gift, the Holy Spirit. Only the power of God's Holy Spirit can keep us clean and useable.**

Sometimes people try to put other stuff in their lives to keep sin out, but it doesn't work. Ask several students to stuff the packing peanuts into their cups. When the cups are full, ask: **Will this keep the mud out?** Ask one student to dip his cup into the mud. **No! The mud still gets inside.** Have several other students stuff their cups full of newspaper. Ask:

★ **What about now? Will the newspaper keep the mud out?**

★ **What would happen if you could keep the mud out but were under some other kind of pressure?**

Ask a few children to crush their cups. Say: **The cup can be crushed. When we are filled with the Holy Spirit, we cannot be crushed.** Have a volunteer read 2 Corinthians 4:8. **The Bible tells us that we are going to have all kinds of pressure and be tempted to get dirty with sin,**

but with the Holy Spirit, we will not be crushed.

Show the children one of the plaster paperweights. Pass the paperweight around. **This cup of plaster represents our lives when we are filled with the Holy Spirit. We might have opportunities to sin, but the Holy Spirit will help us keep the sin out.** Try to pour some of mud into the cup. **Satan may try to hurt us with all kinds of pressure and temptation, but he will not be able to crush us.** Ask the kids to try to crush the cup with their hands.

Distribute the pre-made paperweights, one to each child. **We're going to make some Lamb paperweights. As you decorate your paperweight, think about the joy God feels when we decide to accept his gift of salvation; think about the joy we feel when we have our sins forgiven; and think about the joy we have when we are strengthened by the Holy Spirit in us.**

Ask the children to invert their cups. Help them cut out and glue felt ears to the top of the cup so the ears flop down at the sides. Have them fluff some cotton balls and glue them to the top of the cup. The face and child's name will be added later in the lesson.

THE MESSAGE IN MOTION

Before class, collect self-sealing sandwich bags, plastic spoons, powdered bubble bath, and candy confetti or candy sprinkles. You'll also need tape or a stapler and copies of the Scripture strip for Psalm 119:41 from page 127.

Have kids work in small groups. Distribute the self-sealing sandwich bags and direct kids each to fill their bags about half full of powdered bubble bath. Then have kids measure a spoonful of candy confetti or sprinkles into the bubble-bath powder. As kids work, explain that one or two spoonfuls of this neat bubble bath can be sprinkled under running bath water as kids are filling the tub. Point out how the candy sprinkles will dissolve in the warm water after a bit but that there will be mounds of sparkling bubbles to enjoy. Tell kids the bubbles and colorful candy bits symbolize the joy and celebration we feel in accepting Jesus' gift of salvation.

When the bubble-bath powder and candy bits are in the plastic bag, drop in the plastic spoon for bath-time measuring, then seal the bags. Have kids tape or staple their Scripture strips to the bags.

Say: **Your bubble bath is for cleaning your bodies, but it's also a fun, bubbly reminder of the joy we have in loving Jesus. Only God can clean**

our hearts and spirits when we accept his gift of salvation. Read Ephesians 2:8, 9. **God's Word tells us we're saved by grace, which God offers out of love and which brings joy both to him and to us! Let's see what else God's Word says about being saved as we review our Might Memory Verse.**

SUPER SCRIPTURE

Have kids look at the Scripture strips on their bags of bubble bath and repeat the verse three times in unison. Then challenge pairs of kids to repeat the verse, each person saying a portion. For example, one child will say: "May your unfailing love come to me, O Lord," and another child will say: "Your salvation according to your promise." (If you have older kids and want them to learn the extra-challenge verse, introduce John 14:6 at this time.)

When everyone has had a turn to repeat the verse with a partner, say: **This verse is almost like a prayer. This verse asks the Lord for his love and salvation to come to us. When we accept God's gift of salvation and seek his forgiveness, we're asking for the Lord's love and salvation to come to us too.** Ask:

• **Why is it good to** *invite* **God's love and salvation to come to us instead of being forced to have it?**

• **Why do we need the Lord's love and salvation?**

• **How is seeking God's love and salvation a demonstration of our love? of our faith?**

Say: **Wanting the Lord's love and salvation shows that we love God and choose to obey him. And that puts big, joyful smiles in our hearts and on our faces!** Ask each student to add a smiling face to her sheep as a reminder of the joy of being saved.

A POWERFUL PROMISE

Gather kids in a circle. Say: **We've spent some time learning about the joy that comes from being saved. We've discovered that Jesus wants us to be saved. And we learned that it makes God joyful when we are saved. We also reviewed the Mighty Memory Verse that says** (lead kids in repeating Psalm 119:41), **"May your unfailing love come to me, O Lord, your salvation according to your promise" Psalm 119:41.** (If you're learning the extra-challenge verse, repeat it also.)

Hold up the Bible and say: **The Bible gives us so many reasons to be joyful. Listen to this verse and tell me why we're supposed to rejoice.** Read aloud Luke 10:20b: **"Rejoice that your names are written in heaven."** Invite kids to tell that we can rejoice because our names are written in heaven and because God knows and loves us. Have each child write his name on his sheep as a reminder that our names are written in heaven when we are saved. Say: **The Lord loves us all so very much and wants us to be saved. And we love Jesus so very much and want him to lead our lives. Let's close our time together with a prayer expressing our love and desire to follow Jesus.**

Close with a prayer thanking Jesus for his gift of salvation and for his love that brings us never-ending joy. End with this responsive good-bye:

Leader: **May the joy of Jesus be with you.**

Children: **And also with you!**

Distribute the Power Page! take-home papers as kids are leaving. Thank children for coming and encourage them to thank Jesus for his gifts of love and salvation during the week.

POWER PAGE!

ALL for Love

Read Luke 15:3-6. Number the events in the ❤ shapes in the order they happened. Then fill in the missing word to discover how God feels when one person is saved.

He finds the lost sheep.

A man loses one sheep.

He brings the sheep home.

He looks for the lost sheep.

He leaves the other 99.

" _____ _____ ___ ;

__ _____ _____ ___

_____ _____ " (Luke 15:6).

Important Choice!

Visit with your parents, teacher, or other church leader about what it means to be saved. Read some Bible verses to help you understand God's gift of salvation. Check off the verses when you read them.

- ❏ John 3:16
- ❏ Acts 4:12
- ❏ Acts 16:31-33
- ❏ Romans 10:9, 13
- ❏ Mark 16:16
- ❏ Ephesians 2:8, 9

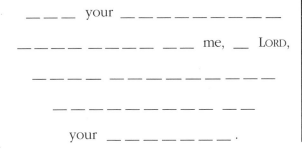

Fill-'em-In

Write **PSALM 119:41** on the spaces below, then fill those words in the puzzle.

____ your _____ ____

_____ ___ me, __ LORD,

____ _____ _____

____ _____

your _____ .

NEVER-CHANGING JOY

Jesus and the joy he offers are unchanging and always present!

Matthew 28:20

Hebrews 13:8

2 John 2, 3

SESSION SUPPLIES

★ Bibles

★ markers

★ tape

★ "old" or worn-out items (see the Power Focus)

★ ice cubes

★ paper towels

★ newsprint

★ photocopies of the Constant or Changing? handout (page 124)

★ photocopies of the Whiz Quiz (page 88) and the Power Page! (page 87)

MIGHTY MEMORY VERSE

May your unfailing love come to me, O LORD, your salvation according to your promise. Psalm 119:41.

(For older kids, add in John 14:6: "I am the way and the truth and the life. No one comes to the Father except through me.")

SESSION OBJECTIVES

During this session, children will

★ discover that Jesus is always with us

★ learn the difference between *temporary* and *constant*

★ realize that Jesus is unchanging and his love constant

★ understand that joy from Christ never fades away

BIBLE BACKGROUND

What can be as frustrating and senseless as "a ceaseless chasing after the wind"? Chasing after promotions, higher pay, bigger houses, fancier cars, and sparkling gems and jewels in the end is as senseless, ceaseless, and temporary as chasing after the wind. Yet how many of us find ourselves enmeshed in the chase even as we recognize the temporal nature of it deep inside our hearts and minds? When we stop to consider those lilies of the field and the grass that blows to chaff, we're reminded that the things that truly count and are constant are all of God and his kingdom. It's these timeless, treasured truths that bring us eternal joy and everlasting love.

Let's face it—kids are often fickle little elves. A new best friend each week, a favorite food every meal, and a new toy to embrace every birthday keep teachers on their toes and parents pursuing changing "wish" lists all year long! Kids don't usually consider the very temporary nature of life, relationships, toys, and such. But inside, they often yearn for constancy in *something* or *someone*. It's vital for kids to learn that the things of the Lord and the Lord himself offer the constancy kids crave. Use this lesson to raise kids' awareness of the temporary nature of earthly things and the joyful constancy of the Lord and his kingdom.

POWER focus

Before class, collect the following items: an old shoe, withered grass or leaves, a dead flower, and an empty cereal box.

Warmly welcome kids and have them gather around the "old" items you brought to class. Set the Bible beside you and say: **Look at all these items. What are they, and what do you think they all have in common?** Allow children to tell their ideas. Suggestions for similarities might include "they're all old," "they're not pretty and new or fresh," and "they aren't useable any longer."

Say: **These items all have one thing in common: they're old or they've withered away. What things can you think of that we use up in our world or that wither away or die?**

Again, encourage kids to share as many suggestions as they can think up, then continue: ***All* things born of our world eventually wither away, die, fade, or become used up. Flowers, grasses, people, foods, clothing, toys, and trees are all what we call "temporary" things because they don't last forever.** Hold up the Bible and say: **But there are some things that are constant and never change, grow old, or fade away.**

Today we'll discover what constants there are in our very temporary world and lives. We'll learn how these constants bring us wonderful joy. And we'll review our Mighty Memory Verse that tells us about the constant love of the Lord and his salvation.

To get started, let's form small groups, and we'll help each other discover what things are temporary and what things are constants in our lives.

THE **MIGHTY** MESSAGE

Before this activity, photocopy the Constant or Changing? handout from page 124. You'll need one copy for each child. You'll also need colorful markers for kids to write and draw with.

After kids are in their small groups, distribute the handouts and markers. Say: **Let's see how good of detectives you are as we read several Bible verses and decide if the Bible is talking about something that changes and is temporary or is constant and stays the same. If you think the verse is about something temporary, draw or write the name of that thing in a flower outline, because flowers are temporary and wither away. If you think the verse is talking about something that is constant and never changes, draw or write the name of that thing in a heart shape.**

Invite a volunteer to read aloud each of the following verses and let kids decide if the verse is referring to something temporary or something constant in nature. Then have kids draw a picture or write the name of the thing in the appropriate flower or heart shape. For example, if a verse speaks of withering grass, draw a picture of brown grass or write the word "grass" in a flower shape to signify that grass is temporary.

★ James 1:11a *(temporary—blossoms)*

★ Hebrews 13:8 *(constant—Jesus)*

★ Psalm 37:38 *(temporary—wicked people)*

★ 2 John 2, 3 *(constant—the truth)*

★ Psalm 129:6 *(temporary—grass)*

★ Matthew 28:20 *(constant—Jesus' presence)*

★ 1 Chronicles 16:34 *(constant—the Lord's love)*

★ Isaiah 40:8 *(temporary—flowers; constant—God's Word)*

When the flower and heart shapes have been filled in, ask:

★ **What kinds of things are temporary and will fade away?**

★ **What kinds of things are constant and unchanging?**

★ **Which things are of God: temporary or constant? Explain.**

★ **Which are more important to our lives: temporary or constant things? Explain.**

POWER POINTERS

Have kids write down feelings they've experienced, then circle the emotions that didn't last long. This helps kids see that joy and faith persevere and help us through temporary tough times!

Say: **There are many things in our lives that are temporary and will fade away. But the really important things never will fade away—they will remain constant forever!** Read aloud Hebrews 13:8 once more, then say: **Jesus is constant, and so are his love, his truth, his salvation, and the joy that comes from following him. Jesus promises to be with us always, and we know he will stay the same today and tomorrow and forever. That gives me great joy that lasts forever too! Let's play a cool relay game to remind us about Jesus' constant love and the never-ending joy he offers us.**

THE MESSAGE IN MOTION

Before class, plan on bringing a tray of ice cubes for this cool relay game. Kids will be passing ice cubes in a circle to see how long they can keep them from melting. You'll also need a roll of paper towels for those drips and drizzles!

Have kids form three or four small groups and hand each child a paper towel. (If your class is very large, form additional groups as needed.) Explain that in this cool relay, kids will be passing ice cubes from hand to hand around the circles to see which team can make their ice cube last the

longest. Tell kids that they must keep the ice cube moving from hand to hand around the circles at all times and if things get a bit too drippy, they can wipe their hands on the paper towels. When a group's ice cube has melted, they must say, "Here today, gone tomorrow!"

When the last group's ice cube has finally melted, have kids sit in a large circle and dry off using the paper towels.
Say: **That was loads of fun! And it was a good reminder how quickly things of this earth fade away—even when we try to make them last a long time! Even if we had passed a rock, sooner or later it would have broken down into little**

pebbles and sand. Some things take longer to change and fade away, but eventually they will. The only lasting things are the Lord's love, his forgiveness, his Word, and the joy that comes from knowing, loving, and following the Lord. Ask:

★ Ice melted away as we passed it. What would happen if we passed Jesus' love and joy to others?

★ Why is it good that Jesus' love and joy never fade away or change?

★ How does it strengthen our faith to know that Jesus is the same yesterday, today, and forever?

Form one large circle and read aloud Hebrews 13:8 once again.

Explain that this time you'll be tossing an ice cube back and forth across the circle. Each time the ice cube is caught, the catcher must say, "Jesus Christ is the same yesterday and today and forever." Continue until everyone has had a turn repeating the verse, then sit in place.

Say: **It makes me feel safe, secure, and very joyous to know that Jesus never changes. I can trust that he will always be with me, always love me, and always guide me to God when I obey him. God's Word teaches us so much about the constancy of Jesus. Remember the verses earlier that spoke of how God's Word and truth last forever? Let's review the Mighty Memory Verse we've been learning as we recognize that it is God's truth that will never fade away either.**

SUPER SCRIPTURE

Before class, write Psalm 119:41 on newsprint. If you've been learning the extra-challenge verse, write it on a piece of newsprint also. Cut the verse papers into as many pieces as there are kids in the class. Set a roll of tape by the wall or a door.

Hand out the puzzle pieces and challenge kids to work silently together to assemble the verse and tape it to the wall or door. When the verse is assembled correctly, take turns challenging one another to repeat the words without peeking at the newsprint. If a child needs help, he can ask a "lifesaver" to give a word or two of the verse. Continue until everyone has had a turn to repeat the verse, then give each other high fives.

Say: **This powerful verse teaches us that the Lord's love is unfailing; in other words, it's always the same and unchanging, just as we've been learning today.** Ask:

★ **How does it help us stay joyful to know that the Lord's love is unfailing and always the same?**

★ **What other things about the Lord are unfailing?** (Suggestions might include God's mercy, grace, forgiveness, presence, and help.)

Say: **It strengthens our faith, trust, hope, and joy to know that the Lord is unfailing in every way. From his truth to his help and constant presence in our lives, we can trust the Lord to be unfailing and unchanging in every way. Let's express our joy to the Lord for his constancy and unchanging nature by singing the Joy Song.**

Lead kids in singing the Joy Song to the tune of Old MacDonald and in the accompanying actions.

JOY SONG

There is joy down in my heart, (point to your heart)
And Jesus put it there! (point upward)
Joy that cannot fade away (shake your finger "no")
And follows everywhere! (turn around in place)
J-O-Y, sign it high— (sign the letters for "joy" two times)
Jump for joy and give high fives! (jump, then give high fives)
There is joy down in my heart, (point to your heart)
And Jesus put it there! (point upward)

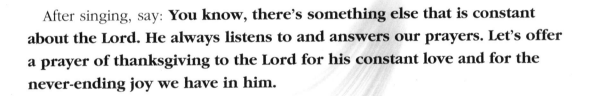

After singing, say: **You know, there's something else that is constant about the Lord. He always listens to and answers our prayers. Let's offer a prayer of thanksgiving to the Lord for his constant love and for the never-ending joy we have in him.**

A **POWERFUL** PROMISE

Gather kids and say: **We've been learning today that Jesus is the same yesterday and today and forever. We've explored the differences between something that is temporary and fades away, such as flowers and grass, and something that is constant, such as Jesus and his truth and love. We've discovered that the joy we have in Jesus is something that never fades away. And we've reviewed the Mighty Memory Verse that says** (repeat Psalm 119:41 and the extra-challenge verse, if you've been learning it), **"May your unfailing love come to me, O Lord, your salvation according to your promise."**

Hold up the Bible and say: **God's Word teaches us about his constancy and how Jesus is always the same. We can try to be always the same in our loving, joyful attitude toward God and others. We'll pass the Bible around the circle. When it's your turn to hold the Bible, you can say, "Please help me have a never-ending attitude of joy, Lord."** Continue passing the Bible until everyone has had a turn to hold it. Then end with a corporate "amen."

Before kids leave, allow five or ten minutes to complete the Whiz Quiz from page 88. If you run out of time, be sure to do this page first thing next week. The Whiz Quiz is an invaluable tool that allows kids, teachers, and parents see what kids have learned in the previous three weeks.

Read aloud 2 John 2, 3. Then close with this responsive good-bye:

Leader: **May Jesus' love, truth, and joy be with you.**

Children: **And also with you!**

Distribute the Power Page! take-home papers as kids are leaving. Thank children for coming and encourage them to thank Jesus for his constant joy this week.

POWER PAGE!

Stay Vs. Go Away

Decide where each of the following would go:
will they fade away or forever stay?

✓ God's love
✓ grass
✓ Jesus' promises
✓ people
✓ fame
✓ God's truth

✓ flowers
✓ God's presence
✓ God's Word
✓ money & jewels
✓ Jesus' salvation
✓ Spirit's help

will always stay

will go away

SWEETEST TREAT

Give each person in your family a jaw-breaker or other hard candy. How long can you make the sweetness last: 3 minutes? 5 minutes? 10 minutes or longer? As you enjoy the sweet treat, name sweet things that stay forever, such as God's Word or Jesus' love.
Then remind your family that the sweetness of Jesus' love, forgiveness, truth, help, and joy last far beyond any jaw-breaker or hard candy! End by reading this verse aloud and giving each other joyous hugs:

"Because of the truth, which lives in us and will be with us forever: Grace, mercy and peace from God the Father and from Jesus Christ, the Father's Son, will be with us in truth and love" (2 John 2, 3).

LETTER BEFORE

Write the letter that comes <u>before</u>
the letter under each space
to complete Psalm 119:41.

__ __ __ __ __ __ __ __ __ __ __ __ __ __ __ __ __ __ __ __ __ __
N B Z   Z P V S   V O G B J M J O H   M P W F   D P N F

__ __ __, __ __ __ __ __, __ __ __ __ __ __ __ __ __ __
U P N F   P M P S E   Z P V S   T B M W B U J P O

__ __ __ __ __ __ __ __ __ __ __ __ __ __ __ __ __ __ __ __ __ __ __
B D D P S E J O H   U P   Z P V S   Q S P N J T F

WHIZ QUIZ

Fill in the word to complete each sentence.

❤ The only way to _____ is through Jesus.

❤ Jesus is the way and the truth and the _____.

❤ _____ was baptized to obey his Father.

❤ Our _____ are written in heaven.

❤ Joy from Jesus is _____.

❤ Jesus is with us _____!

WORD BANK

Jesus

names

God

forever

life

constant

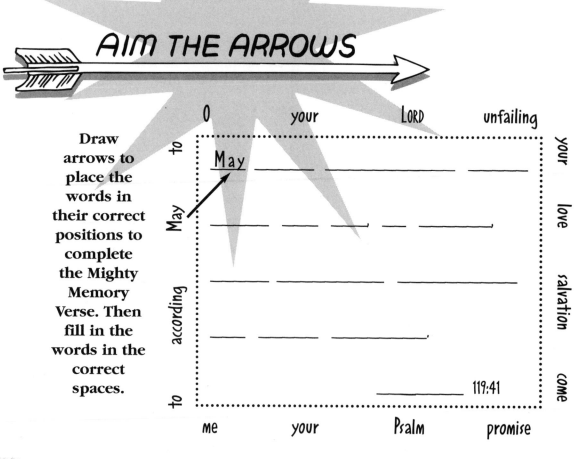

AIM THE ARROWS

Draw arrows to place the words in their correct positions to complete the Mighty Memory Verse. Then fill in the words in the correct spaces.

O   your   LORD   unfailing

to   May _____ _____ _____ your

May   _____ _____ _____ love

according   _____ _____ salvation

            _____ _____ come

to   _____ 119:41

me   your   Psalm   promise

JOY THROUGH CHOOSING JESUS

For you make me glad by your
deeds, O LORD; I sing for joy
at the works of your hands.
Psalm 92:4

HAPPY OR JOYFUL?

Joy is different from happiness—and more constant!

Psalms 20:5; 21:6;
28:7; 68:3
1 Thessalonians 5:16

SESSION SUPPLIES

★ Bibles
★ newsprint
★ permanent markers
★ scissors
★ construction paper
★ tacky craft glue & tape
★ white shower-curtain liners
★ white shelf paper and stiff paper
★ colorful magazines
★ photocopies of the Power Page! (page 97)

MIGHTY MEMORY VERSE

For you make me glad by your deeds, O LORD; I sing for joy at the works of your hands. Psalm 92:4

SESSION OBJECTIVES

During this session, children will
★ understand the differences between happiness and joy
★ realize that happiness depends on situations
★ know that joy from Jesus is constant
★ learn that joy involves action

BIBLE BACKGROUND

Think back to emotions you've experienced in the past twenty-four hours. Chances are, you traveled through a wide gamut of feelings ranging from happy, tired, and pleased to surprised, peaceful, and possibly irritated. We change our feelings more often than chameleons change their colors on confetti! Situations, relationships, and our own perception of life color our feelings and keep them in constant motion. Is there any feeling that lasts through thick and thin, good times and bad? Yes, the joy we have through knowing, loving, and following Jesus is enduring joy that cannot be taken away. How wonderful that through our changing array of emotions and situations, joy in Jesus stays bright and beautiful!

If adult emotions change like the wind, kids' feelings change with the speed of light! One moment they love their new skates, then after a fall, they can't stand them. Wait yet another moment, and they're happily gliding along the sidewalk. Kids find it hard to understand how we can have joy at the same time we feel sad. They need to learn that happiness, sadness, and other emotions simply live on our faces for a while, but joy from Jesus lives and lasts in our hearts. Use this lively lesson to help kids discover the differences between temporary feelings and joy from Jesus that is constant.

POWER FOCUS

Before class, enlarge and redraw the faces from the margin on sheets of newsprint. Tape the faces to the wall or a door. Cut out seven 3-inch red paper hearts and keep all but one hidden for most of the activity.

Warmly welcome kids to class and gather them in front of the faces on the wall. Hold one paper heart (but keep the others hidden in your pocket or behind you) and say: **Here are some faces to greet us today. Look over the faces carefully. What does each face show?** Invite kids to tell that the faces express confusion, anger, sadness, surprise, sleepiness, and happiness.

Then say: **Which face shows joy? When you think you know, place your hand over your heart.** Choose a child with her hand on her heart to tape the paper heart under the face she thinks shows joy.

Say: **Raise your hand if you agree with that choice.** Pause for responses, then continue. Then say: **Well, you are correct. The smiley face shows joy—but so do the other faces!** Tape paper hearts below the remainder of the faces.

Say: **I see some surprised faces! Did you know that it's possible to have joy at the same time that we're sad or sleepy or maybe even angry? We can have joy and happiness or sadness at the same time because they come from difference places! We have many** *feelings,* **such as happiness, sadness, anger, or surprise, and those feelings can change often throughout the day and night. One moment we might be**

happy to hear soft rain falling, but that can change in a flash if friends call and want to play outside. Or perhaps you think your new skates are great until you fall and skin your knee.

Feelings such as happiness, sadness, anger, confusion, and surprise live on our faces, but only for moments at a time. Joy, on the other hand, is deeper. It lives in our hearts and spirits because of loving Jesus! As we learned last week, joy from Jesus doesn't change. It's constant and enduring and lasts through happy times, sad times, and moments of frustration or confusion.

Today we'll discover more about the differences between being *happy* and wanting to jump for *joy.* We'll review how things like happiness or sadness are temporary and how joy is constant. And we'll begin learning a new Mighty Memory Verse that teaches us the difference between expressing happiness and expressing true joy. But right now, let's discover the real difference joy makes in our lives and how it is different from just being happy.

POWER POINTERS

Help kids better understand the difference between temporary and constant by explaining that it may be sunny one moment and raining the next, but there's always air present to make weather.

THE MIGHTY MESSAGE

Before class, cut out a large paper doll for every five or six kids—the larger the better! Use white shelf paper for "almost life-size" paper dolls (or use newspaper and add copy-paper heads). Add facial features but omit the mouths. Cut a large paper heart for each paper doll but do not attach them.

You'll also need to cut out a large smiling mouth from a color magazine picture for each paper figure. (You'll need magazines for the next activity, so collect several.) Glue the magazine smiles to stiff paper. Kids will be attaching and reattaching the hearts and mouths to the paper dolls in this activity. (Use rolled tape behind the paper mouths and hearts.) Tape the paper dolls to the wall and set the paper smiles and hearts under them.

Gather kids in groups of five or six and have them sit in front of the paper dolls. Say: **I'll read some verses about happiness or gladness and joy. If you think the verse talks about happiness that lives on our faces, tape a** paper smile to your group's paper doll. If you think the verse talks about joy that lives in our hearts, tape a paper heart to your doll. And if you think the verse talks of both, tape both a heart and smile to your paper figure.

Read aloud the following verses and have kids decide if the verse talks about happiness or joy or both. After each verse, have kids tell why they chose the response they chose. Caution kids to tape and untape the paper features carefully to avoid tears.

★ Psalm 20:5 *(joy)*
★ Proverbs 23:15 *(happiness)*
★ Psalm 21:6 *(both happiness and joy)*
★ Luke 15:32 *(happiness)*
★ Psalm 90:14 *(both happiness and joy)*
★ Psalm 28:7 *(joy)*
★ Psalm 68:3 *(both happiness and joy)*

After reading the verses, say: **Just as these verses teach, sometimes we feel happiness or gladness, yet we also have nonstop joy when we love the Lord! We can be glad *and* rejoice. We can be happy *and* shout for joy. And even though we may feel sadness at times, the joy that lives in our hearts stays in place and doesn't leave.**

★ **Why is it good to know that the joy we have from the Lord stays in our hearts no matter what?**
★ **How does having constant joy in our hearts help us overcome hard times?**
★ **In what ways is joy related to faith and hope?**

Say: **Happiness, sadness, surprise, confusion, frustration, anger, and other emotions are just temporary and will change at any time. They live on our faces. But joy from Jesus lives in our hearts and is constant no matter what! I can feel sad but also have deep joy in my heart and recognize that the sadness will go away in time. That gives me hope and makes me feel wonderful!**

Invite a volunteer to read aloud Psalm 20:5 once more. Then say: **When we feel joy from the Lord and all he does for us, it makes us want to express that joy actively. This verse tells us of expressing joy through shouting and lifting our banners high with the Lord's victory! Let's express our joy by making neat banners to lift high.**

THE MESSAGE IN MOTION

Before class, collect colorful magazines that have pictures of people smiling. Kids will be cutting the smiles from the faces and adding them to their banners. You'll also need to collect permanent markers, scissors, tacky craft glue, construction paper, and one white plastic shower-curtain liner for every eight kids. Cut the shower-curtain liners in eight equal parts. Write the words to the Joy Rap from this activity on newsprint and tape the words to the wall for kids to read.

Invite kids to work in pairs or small groups and distribute the shower-curtain sections. For each banner, have kids write "We will SHOUT for joy—" across the top and "We will LIFT our banners!" across the bottom. Use permanent markers so the ink won't run. (Kids may wish to use pencils to write the letters before tracing them with permanent ink!) Next, have kids draw large faces across the centers of the banners but omit the mouths. Then invite kids to cut colorful, smiling mouths from magazine pic-

tures and glue them to the faces on the banner. The effect is cool, colorful, and comical—kids will love it!

Finally, cut a paper heart to glue in place below each smiling face. Remind kids that joy lives in our

hearts, and the paper hearts signify the joy we feel and want to express.

When the banners are complete, have kids hold them high and look at each other's smiling, joyous faces. Then say: **Happiness is a feeling that lives on our faces and may only last a while. Joy lives in our hearts and cannot be taken away. Joy also creates action in us, as in "jumping for joy," "shouting for joy," or "singing and rejoicing." Let's express our joy in another active way. We can learn a new Joy Rap to express the love and joy we have for the Lord.**

Lead kids in repeating the words to the Joy Rap and encourage them to make up accompanying actions to the words.

JOY RAP

I may be happy for a little while;
I may give a grin or a sunny smile.
But happiness only lives on my face;
It's the joy in my HEART that stays in place!

Chorus:
Oh, I've got . . .
Hand-clappin', finger-snappin',
Foot-stompin', joy-jumpin',
Tail-waggin', Jesus-braggin' JOY!

I may be sad that it's rainy outside;
I may frown and feel down and wanna hide.
But sadness only lives on my face;
It's the joy in my HEART that stays in place!
(Repeat chorus)

After the rap, say: **Wow! It's great expressing joy in lively ways! Let's see what our new Mighty Memory Verse teaches us about wanting to express joy in lively ways.**

SUPER SCRIPTURE

Before this activity, enlarge and draw the Scripture picture for Psalm 92:4, using the illustration as a guide. Hang the verse where kids can see it.

Gather kids in front of the Scripture picture. Repeat the verse three times as you point to

the words on the picture. Say: **This awesome verse teaches us about the difference between feeling happy and being joyful at what God does for us. See how the first part of the verse tells about making us glad? There is a smile to show gladness, but there's not lots of action or expression. That comes next! The second part of the verse speaks of singing for joy**

and expressing joy in a lively way. **Both parts tell of the gladness and joy we get from the Lord and what he does.** Ask:

★ **In what ways can we express joy?**

★ **Why do you think joy is more active than just feeling happy or glad?**

★ **How can you express joy to the Lord this week?**

Repeat the verse two more times aloud. Then say: **Let's express our joy through singing, just as the verse says. We can sing the Joy Song we learned several weeks ago.** Lead kids in singing the Joy Song (page 17) to the tune of Old MacDonald.

Say: **Happiness is a temporary feeling that lives on our faces, but joy is an attitude that lives in our hearts and is constant because it's from the Lord. Let's joyously express our thanks for joy and love from Jesus by offering him a prayer. We'll need our banners to raise.**

Keep the Scripture picture to use next week.

A POWERFUL PROMISE

Have kids stand in a large circle holding their banners. Say: **We've learned today that there is a difference between feeling** *happy* **and living in** *joy.* **We've discovered that happiness and other emotions live on our faces and can change in a flash but that joy from Jesus lives in our hearts forever. And we've explored ways to express joy.**

Read aloud Psalm 28:7, then say: **Our joy comes from the strength, love, and power of the Lord. No wonder it is permanent and lives inside our hearts! Let's bow our heads as we pray. Then you can lift your banner high and joyously shout out the words on it.** Pray: **Dear Lord, we thank you for the wondrous works of your hands and for the love and strength you give us. And to show you our love and joy . . .** (lead kids in shouting out the words from their banners, then end with a corporate "amen").

Read aloud 1 Thessalonians 5:16 and close with this responsive good-bye:

Leader: **May you always feel the victory of Jesus' joy.**

Children: **And also you!**

Distribute the Power Page! take-home papers as kids are leaving. Thank children for coming and encourage them to hang their banners at home to remind everyone of the joy that lives in our hearts and lives through Jesus.

POWER PAGE!

Where Joy Lives!

Use your Bible to fill in the missing words to Psalm 68:3. Then solve the bottom puzzle to learn where joy lives.

"But may the _ _ _ _ _ _ _
                8   10 7

be _ _ _ _ and _ _ _ _ _ _
      1   5   3

before God; may they be _ _ _ _ _ _
                         6 0   9

and _ _ _ _ _ _ _ ."
    2   4   11

Happiness only lives on your

_ _ _ _ , but _ _ _ in
4 1 3 7   2 5 9

your _ _ _ _ _ stays in
     6 7 1 8 10

_ _ _ _ _ !
0 11 1 3 7

MAGNETIC JOY

Make a neat set of emotion magnets to help express your feelings.

Whatcha need:

✓ 5 plastic spoons   ✓ ribbon
✓ sticky magnetic tape
✓ permanent markers

Whatcha do:

(1) Draw faces on the spoons to show common emotions: happy, sad, surprise, angry, confused. **(2)** Draw a ❤ on each spoon to show we still have joy no matter how we feel. **(3)** Tie ribbons to the spoons. Add a piece of sticky magnetic tape behind each spoon "head." **(4)** Hang the spoons on your refrigerator as a reminder of the constancy of God's joy.

SCRIPTURE SCRAMBLER

Unscramble the words in the word bank to complete Psalm 92:4

_ _ _ _ _ _ _ _ _ _ me _ _ _ _

_ _ _ _ _ _ _ _ , O _ _ _ _ _ ;

I _ _ _ _ _ _ _ _ _ at _ _ _

_ _ _ _ _ of _ _ _ _ _ _ _ _ .

WORD BANK

ruoy   *yjo*

ryuo   *Fro*

yb   *algd*

shand   *ededs*

oLrd   *uyo*

kwors   *kame*

rfo   *igns*

teb

JOY IN THE CHOICE

Joy is a matter of choice—and choosing Jesus!

Joshua 24:15
Psalm 33:21
Isaiah 7:15
Romans 12:12-15

SESSION SUPPLIES

★ Bibles
★ fresh fruit & spoiled fruit
★ paper towels
★ tape & scissors
★ paper plates and napkins
★ crispy taco shells
★ choices for filling tacos (see Message in Motion)
★ small plastic apples
★ white paint pens
★ photocopies of the poem on page 104
★ photocopies of the Choices strips (page 101)
★ photocopies of the Power Page! (page 105)

MIGHTY MEMORY VERSE

For you make me glad by your deeds, O Lord; I sing for joy at the works of your hands. Psalm 92:4

(For older kids, add in Psalm 28:7a: "The Lord is my strength and my shield; my heart trusts in him, and I am helped.")

SESSION OBJECTIVES

During this session, children will
★ realize that joy is a choice we make each day
★ understand that choosing Jesus brings joy
★ discover ways to choose joy over trials
★ explore how choosing joy affects our lives

BIBLE BACKGROUND

Why are we so adept at the often unhealthy choices we make? Chocolate may not be the healthiest choice for a snack, but it tastes *so* good. Thank goodness that most choices we make are not life-altering or affecting! Still, there is one choice that *is* life-changing, and that is the choice we make to accept Jesus into our lives. The Bible tells us over and over that we are a chosen people, but real joy comes when *we* choose to love and obey Jesus each day of our lives. Isn't it wonderful that such a powerful, life-affecting choice is there for everyone to choose and embrace?

Kids love choices and being able to decide for themselves what to eat, which shirt to wear, or how to style their hair. Choices build autonomy and self-sufficiency as well as teach how all decisions have consequences. Kids need to understand that the choice they make of whom to love, follow, accept, and worship has eternal consequences and joyous rewards when the right choice is made. Use this important lesson to help kids realize that accepting Jesus is the most important choice they'll ever make.

POWER FOCUS

Before class, choose apples or other fruits to set out for kids to choose to eat. Cut the fruits in quarters and choose both good pieces and rotten pieces. Be sure you have a good piece of fruit for each child, since this is the fruit kids will ultimately choose to eat.

Warmly welcome kids to class and distribute paper towels. Show kids the fruit and say: **To kick off our time together, let's choose a good snack to nibble. Look over the fruit and choose a piece you'd like to eat, then find a place to sit down.** Don't say anything that would affect the choices kids are making—let them choose of their own free will.

When kids are seated with their fruit, say: **You all made your choices, but before we eat our fruit, let's see why you chose the fruit you chose.** Encourage kids to go around the room and explain the reason behind their choices. Explanations might include "because the other fruit was icky," "the other pieces were rotten," and "this fruit was the best." Ask:

★ **In what ways was choosing fruit like making choices in our lives?**

★ **Why do we steer clear of making poor choices?**

★ **How does it help to make good, healthy choices?**

Invite kids to nibble their fruit as you read aloud Isaiah 7:15. Say: **We all make choices each day. Some of them don't matter a whole lot, such as what color shoes to wear or how to style our hair. But other choices can affect our lives and the attitudes we have, such as making decisions of right or wrong or choosing who to be friends with. Just as you chose good fruit, we want to choose good things in our lives.**

Joy is a choice we make each day too. Choosing joy over feeling cranky, angry, or hopeless can make the difference between having a positive day or a negative one. And choosing Jesus is key in choosing joy!

Today we'll discover what it means to choose joy and how it affects our lives and attitudes. We'll learn that choosing to know, love, and follow Jesus is the first step in choosing joy. And we'll

review our Mighty Memory Verse as we explore ways to choose joy in our lives. Right now, let's see what decisions you'd make in some real-life situations!

THE **MIGHTY** MESSAGE

Before class, make a copy of the Choices strips from page 101. Cut apart the situation strips. If your class is very large, make two copies and cut them apart.

Have kids get into six small groups and let them scatter around the room. (If you're using two sets of situation strips, form twelve small groups.) Say: **There are different situations written on these paper strips. They're situations that require an important choice. Read the situation aloud in your group, then decide with your group what you would choose and why. Talk it over and discuss the reasons for your choices. Then after a few moments I'll say "switch," and we'll pass each other different situation strips. When all the groups have read each situation and made their choices, we'll report back to the whole class.**

Allow several minutes to read and discuss each situation before switching strips among groups. When six rotations have been made, call kids back to one group and read aloud each situation. Have groups briefly tell what choices they made and why. For each consensus, have kids give each other high fives. Then ask:

★ **How do our choices affect our relationships with others? the way we feel? our relationship with God?**

★ **In what ways does choosing joy keep us happy? keep us close to Jesus?**

★ **Which do you think comes first: choosing Jesus or choosing joy? Explain.**

Say: **The Bible teaches us that we have an important choice to make: who we will follow and serve.** Read aloud Joshua 24:15. Then continue: **We must first choose to love, serve, follow, and embrace Jesus in our lives. Then we can choose to take hold of the joy that Jesus offers us through his love, forgiveness, and salvation. Choosing Jesus comes first, but choosing joy is the important second choice we can make! And wow,**

POWER POINTERS

Brainstorm with kids positive results of making the choice to follow Jesus. Suggestions might include joy, blessings, Jesus' forgiveness, help, love, and his lasting presence.

does that choice make a difference in our attitudes and life! Invite volunteers to read aloud Romans 12:12-15.

Say: **When we choose Jesus and joy in our lives, we become more patient, more happy, and more hopeful. We're better able to help others, serve God, and pray. Choosing to hold on to joy is one of the most important choices we can make. Now let's have a bit of fun with a few more choices as we visit our choice Veggie Taco Bar!**

CHOICES

1. Someone at school has been saying mean things about you. What do you do?
   a. say mean stuff back
   b. get angry, do nothing
   c. make friends with that person

2. You've been grounded for getting home late for dinner. What do you do?
   a. argue, complain
   b. admit you're wrong
   c. stomp to your room

3. God answered a prayer in a way you wish he wouldn't have. What do you do?
   a. accept with thankfulness
   b. quit praying
   c. get angry at God

4. You have a big test and have to skip baseball to study. What do you do?
   a. crab, get mad
   b. cheat on the test, don't study
   c. study with a positive attitude

5. Your friend put a scratch on your new skates. What do you do?
   a. forgive and be kind
   b. wreck her new bike
   c. stay quiet and angry

6. You wake up feeling grumpy and don't even know why. What do you do?
   a. gripe about breakfast
   b. frown and slam the door
   c. smile and be pleasant

THE MESSAGE IN MOTION

Before class, choose a variety of vegetables, cheeses, and sauce toppings for a taco bar. You might include shredded cheese and lettuce, chopped tomatoes, onions, carrots, celery chunks, and olives. Sauces might include picante or even salad dressings. Be sure you have a crispy taco shell for each child. (Add in flour tortillas for even more choice!) Place the food items in bowls or on paper plates. Set out napkins and paper plates.

Let kids take a trip through your Veggie Taco Bar and prepare a taco of their choice. Encourage kids to think about the choices they're making and to be ready to explain the reasons for their choices.

As kids are enjoying their treats, ask them to tell why they made the choices they did. Then say: **These were fun choices that probably didn't matter too much, unless a certain food makes you ill. But all choices, no matter how big or small, can affect our lives and the choice we make to follow Jesus and embrace the joy he offers us each day.**

Invite several volunteers to read aloud Psalm 33:21; Habakkuk 3:18; and Psalm 28:7. Say: **Choosing Jesus and choosing joy makes me want to express the way I feel! Let's rap out the Joy Rap we learned last week to express the joy we have in choosing Jesus.**

JOY RAP

I may be happy for a little while;
I may give a grin or a sunny smile.
But happiness only lives on my face;
It's the joy in my HEART that stays in place!

Chorus:
Oh, I've got …
Hand-clappin', finger-snappin',
Foot-stompin', joy-jumpin',
Tail-waggin', Jesus-braggin' JOY!

I may be sad that it's rainy outside;
I may frown and feel down and wanna hide.
But sadness only lives on my face;
It's the joy in my HEART that stays in place!
(Repeat chorus)

After the Joy Rap, say: **Isn't it great that the choice we make to follow Jesus and hold on to the joy he offers is a choice that always turns out wonderfully well? God's Word teaches us about the wonderful effects of choosing joy. Let's review the Mighty Memory Verse as we explore more about what choosing joy means in our lives.**

SUPER SCRIPTURE

Before class, purchase plastic apples. Apple ornaments are easy to find and inexpensive, but other kinds of plastic apples will work. Be sure the apples are large enough for kids to write "Choose Joy!" on. You'll also need white paint pens, tape, and copies of the poem box from page 104. Be sure the Scripture picture from last week is still on the wall.

Gather kids by the Scripture pictures and have pairs of kids take turns each repeating one portion of Psalm 92:4. Then repeat the verse two times in unison. (If you want to learn the extra-challenge verse, introduce it at this time.)

Say: **This wonderful verse reminds us that joy comes from the Lord and from what he does. The Bible tells us that we are chosen by the Lord to be his special people. Now that gives me great joy! But *we* must also choose God in return, choosing to love and follow him all our lives. God sets joy before us through all that he does for us, and it's up to us to take hold of that awesome joy and hold on to it! Joy keeps negative feelings and doubts away and keeps open the lines of loving the Lord.**

You probably remember that old saying about apples: "An apple a day keeps the doctor away." Well, choosing joy each day keeps doubts and sadness away! Let's make neat fruity reminders that choosing joy from Jesus chases away the negative things in our lives.

Distribute the small plastic apples. Have kids use white paint pens to write "Choose Joy!" on their apples. Then tape a Choose Joy poem box to the hanger, leaf, stem, or side of each apple. Read the poem aloud and briefly discuss how choosing joy keeps negative things from overtaking our attitudes and faith.

Say: **Place your apple reminders in a place where you'll see them often and be reminded that choosing joy each day keeps us healthy, happy, and hopeful! Now let's end with a prayer thanking Jesus for the joy he sets before us.**

A POWERFUL PROMISE

Gather kids in a circle. Say: **We've had a fun time exploring what it means to choose joy in our lives and how choosing joy affects our attitudes and the way we live. We've discovered that choosing Jesus is the key step in choosing joy. And we've reviewed the Mighty Memory Verse that says** (lead kids in repeating Psalm 92:4 and the extra-challenge verse, if you're learning it), **"For you make me glad by your deeds, O Lord; I sing for joy at the works of your hands."**

Hold up the Bible and read aloud Joshua 24:15b. Say: **God's Word tells us of the importance of choosing for ourselves who we choose to follow and serve. We'll pass the Bible around the circle. When it's your turn to hold the Bible, you can say, "I choose Jesus, and I choose joy!"** Continue passing the Bible until everyone has had a turn to hold it, then close with a corporate "amen."

Read aloud Philippians 2:1, 2. Then end with this responsive good-bye:

Leader: **May you choose Jesus and his joy each day.**

Children: **And also you!**

Distribute the Power Page! take-home papers as kids are leaving. Thank children for coming and encourage them to choose Jesus and joy in prayer each morning during the coming week.

Choosing Jesus' JOY each day
Keeps the sadness & doubts away!
(Read Psalm 33:21)

POWER PAGE!

YOU DECIDE!

There are so many important decisions we have to make! Read the verses on the left and match them to the choices on the right.

Deut. 30:19, 20

Rom. 12:12

Col. 2:6

Josh. 24:15

Choose Jesus

Choose God

Choose life

Choose joy

Choose-n-Chews

Choose a night this week to have Family Choice Night.
Set out the buffet below and let family members choose their favorite foods. Then choose several games to play. Remind your family that choosing Jesus to love and obey is the most important choice we make every day!

AWESOME FUN!

Pizza Buffet:
- flour tortillas
- shredded cheese
- pepperoni slices
- mushrooms
- pineapple
- pizza sauce
- onions
- green pepper
- grapes
- apple slices

High & LOW

Fill in the missing high, low, and in-between letters to complete Psalm 92:4.

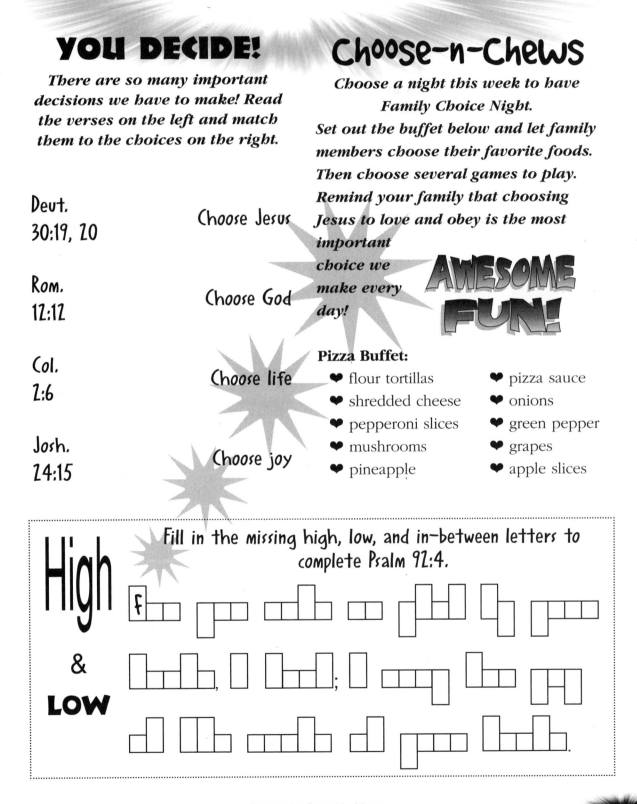

HEAVENLY JOY!

Joy in our heavenly home will shine the brightest!

Revelation 7:15-17;
12:12; 21:4, 5, 23

SESSION SUPPLIES

★ Bibles
★ a small lamp without the shade
★ a box to fit over the lamp
★ a pen & permanent markers (pastel, if possible)
★ 40-watt light bulbs
★ white shelf paper
★ bubble wrap
★ tape & scissors
★ photocopies of the rebus pictures (page 125)
★ photocopies of the Whiz Quiz (page 114) and the Power Page! (page 113)

MIGHTY MEMORY VERSE

For you make me glad by your deeds, O LORD; I sing for joy at the works of your hands. Psalm 92:4
(For older kids, add in Psalm 28:7a: "The LORD is my strength and my shield; my heart trusts in him, and I am helped.")

SESSION OBJECTIVES

During this session, children will
★ discover that joy goes on forever
★ realize that joy in heaven is the brightest of all
★ understand that there will be no negative things in heaven
★ learn that Jesus will be at the center of their heavenly joy

BIBLE BACKGROUND

How many of us wear sunglasses to block the blinding brightness of the sun? Even on cloudy days when there's only a glare, we protect our eyes from the bright light. Now imagine a light so bright it can burn away all the negatives in the world but yet so glorious that it does not blind us. That's what the book of Revelation promises us the new heaven and earth will be like. No blinders to block light or love or joy. God's power and Jesus' brilliant love will shine through as we express our immeasurable joy through praising and singing. In heaven, we'll toss away the sunglasses, blinders, and clouds that often block today's joy and let the light of God's love shine through!

Kids are temporal beings who often have trouble looking toward or planning for the future. They see what's before them, derive joy or sadness from the moment, and don't look toward tomorrow with much more than a passing glance at the calendar. How wonderful it is, then, to teach kids that God's tomorrows are filled with more joy than they can imagine today, where there is no longer sadness, illness, frustrations, anger, or anything other than the blindingly bright light of love and unfettered joy. Use this joyous lesson to teach kids that if joy is good now, our heavenly joy will be *awesome* tomorrow!

POWER FOCUS

Before class, plug in a small lamp and cover it with a box. Turn the lamp on just before kids arrive. In addition, make sure you have markers and a pen handy.

Warmly welcome kids and gather them around the table with the lamp. Say: **We've been spending several weeks learning about the joy that Jesus offers us and how that joy never fades away. We've also discovered how situations sometimes cloud our joy. What are some negative things in our lives and world that often cloud joy?** As kids name things such as anger, world hunger, poverty, illness, and sadness, use the markers to write their ideas on the box.

Hold the pen and say: **Even though there are things in our lives and in this world that cloud over or try to block joy, joy can shine through.** Poke a hole through each negative listed on the box and let the light of the lamp shine through. Then continue: **Wouldn't it be wonderful if we could remove all the blocks and clouds to joy and let the light of joy *really* shine through at its brightest?**

Remove the box from over the lamp and say: **Wow! Now that's bright! Today we'll discover that the joy that waits for us in heaven is the brightest joy ever because there are no negatives to get in the way of its shining. We'll learn who is at the center of this brilliant joy. And we'll review the Mighty Memory Verse that teaches us who all joy comes from. But first let's read about what life will be like in heaven as we learn more about heavenly joy and why it's so bright.** Turn off the lamp.

THE **MIGHTY** MESSAGE

Before class, make three enlarged photocopies of the rebus pictures from page 125 and cut them out. (You'll have a few extra pictures, but this will ensure that you have all that you need.) Cut four 2-foot lengths of white shelf paper and tape them to the wall or floor. (If you have a very large class, tape sheets of shelf paper together to make posters that are 2-by-3-foot. Then photocopy and enlarge the rebus pictures so kids can see them more clearly.) Write the following words (from Revelation 7:15, 17; 21: 4, 5, 23) on the paper, leaving a 4-inch space where indicated. Kids will be adding the rebus pictures to these spaces during the activity. Write each of the following paragraphs on a different sheet of shelf paper:

Therefore, they are before the [space] *of* [space] *and serve him* [space] *and* [space] *in his temple; and he who sits on the* [space] *will spread his* [space] *over them. (Revelation 7:15)*

For the [space] *at the center of the throne will be their* [space]; *he will lead them to springs of living water. And* [space] *will wipe away every* [space] *from their* [space]. *(Revelation 7:17)*

He will wipe every [space] *from their* [space]. *There will be no more* [space] *or* [space] *or* [space]. ... *He who was seated on the* [space] *said, "I am making everything new!" (from Revelation 21:4a, 5a)*

The city does not need the [space] *or the* [space] *to shine on it, for the glory of* [space] *gives it light, and the* [space] *is its* [space]. *(Revelation 21:23)*

Gather kids in front of the four sheets of shelf paper with the words from Revelation on them. Place a roll of tape and the rebus pictures in a pile under the papers on the wall. Say: **The Bible's last book is the book of Revelation. Doesn't the word *Revelation* sound like the word *revealed*? That's because in this book, God reveals to us what heaven and the new earth will be like. It's very exciting to see what God has planned for us when we live with him. I've written several verses from Revelation on these papers, but some of the words are missing.** (Point to the spaces.) **We'll be adding pictures to represent the missing words as we read these verses. And when we're done, you'll know what heavenly joy the Lord has planned for us.**

POWER POINTERS

Let kids use glow-in-the-dark or neon paints to paint their impressions of heavenly joy. Hang the pictures on a bulletin board surrounded by Christmas-tree lights for an awesome display!

Invite a volunteer to read Revelation 7:15 from the Bible. Then have kids decide which pictures fill the spaces and tape them in place. (Have kids use their Bibles if needed.) Continue in the same way until all the verses have been read and the pictures filled in. Then re-read the verses once more in their entirety. Ask:

★ **Why won't we need sunlight or moonlight in the new heaven and earth?**

★ **Who will sit on the throne and give us joyous light and love?**

★ **In what ways is the new heaven and earth different from the "old" one we live in?**

★ **Who will wipe away every tear and bit of sadness?**

★ **Why will joy shine forth so brightly?**

Say: **The Bible tells us that in heaven there will be no more pain or sadness or suffering or crying. In other words, there**

"THEREFORE, THEY ARE BEFORE THE [throne] OF [GOD] AND SERVE HIM [sun] AND [moon] IN HIS TEMPLE; AND HE WHO SITS ON THE [throne] WILL SPREAD HIS [tent] OVER THEM." REVELATION 7:15

will be no more negative things in heaven to block our joy or cloud it over. The joy from Jesus will shine through brighter than even the sun or moon! Just think of it— constant joy that shines brighter than anything we could imagine.

If there's time, form four groups and let kids color the rebus pictures to the verses. Hang the verses back in order on the wall and invite each group to read aloud in unison the verse they colored. Leave the verses in place to read next week.

Say: **Let's explore more about this incredible heavenly joy we can look forward to as we make Bright Joy-Lights to shine in our lamps at home. They'll remind everyone that our future joy will outshine the brightest lights or happiness we know today!**

THE MESSAGE IN MOTION

Before class, collect permanent markers in a variety of colors. Pastel colors will look beautiful when lit up, but basic colors will also work well. You'll also need a 40-watt light bulb for each child and bubble wrap in which to send the bulbs home.

Have kids form pairs or small groups, then explain that kids will be decorating light bulbs using permanent markers. Tell kids to consider using designs that express the joy they feel in looking forward to joyous lives with Jesus. Hearts, stars, clouds, swirls, and words such as "love," "Jesus," or "joy" would work well. Point out that the bulbs will shine beautifully the more they're colored.

As kids decorate their Bright Joy-Lights, visit about what it would be like to live without the negative things we face in the world and our lives, such as fear, anger, frustration, grades in school, illness, and world hate and poverty. Discuss how God's plan for perfect joy gives us hope, strengthens our faith, and helps us persevere through trying times.

When the Bright Joy-Lights are finished, try each one in the lamp you used earlier. Then wrap the bulbs in bubble wrap to carry safely home. Tell kids the Bright Joy-Lights can be used with or without a lamp shade. Encourage kids to gather their families around a lamp using a Bright Joy-Light bulb (without a lamp shade) and visit about our future heavenly joy and how it helps us get through hard times today with joy and hope.

Say: **Your Bright Joy-Lights are awesome and beautiful reminders of the bright joy awaiting us in heaven. God's plans for our future are so bright *and* perfect, but so are the things he does for us today. Let's review our Mighty Memory Verse as we're reminded of the joy we feel in God's deeds and through the works of his hands.** Set aside the bulbs to carry home later.

SUPER SCRIPTURE

Be sure you have the Scripture picture of Psalm 92:4 from last week (or make another, if you need to). Have the lamp set up and ready to turn on and off for this activity.

Seat kids in a circle and hold up the Scripture picture. Repeat the verse in unison two times, then say: **We've been learning how God's deeds and the works of his hands give us joy. Today we've been exploring the bright**

light of joy that will be ours someday in heaven. Let's combine the two to help us remember Psalm 92:4. We'll pass the verse around the circle. When I switch the light on, stop passing. Whoever is holding the verse can hold it high in the air for everyone to see as that person repeats the verse. If you need help repeating it, you can call on a friend to help.

Continue passing the verse and having kids repeat it until everyone has had a turn. (If you've been learning the extra-challenge verse, have kids repeat it now in the same way.) Then ask:

★ **How do God's great deeds and his wondrous works give us joy?**

★ **Is God's plan for our heavenly joy a wondrous work? Explain.**

Read aloud Revelation 5:13. Say: **The Bible tells us that in the new heaven and earth, there will be constant singing and praising of the Lord. We've learned that joy is to be expressed and that one of the ways to express joy is through singing. Even our Mighty Memory Verse tells us about singing for joy to the Lord. Let's sing the Joy Song as we express our joy at all God does and all he has planned for our heavenly home.**

Lead kids in singing the Joy Song to the tune of Old MacDonald and in the accompanying actions.

JOY SONG

There is joy down in my heart, (point to your heart)
And Jesus put it there! (point upward)
Joy that cannot fade away (shake your finger "no")
And follows everywhere! (turn around in place)
J-O-Y, sign it high— (sign the letters for "joy" two times)
Jump for joy and give high fives! (jump, then give high fives)
There is joy down in my heart, (point to your heart)
And Jesus put it there! (point upward)

After singing, say: **What awesome joy we have today through Jesus. And what bright joy we will have in our heavenly home. Let's end our time together by prayerfully thanking the Lord for his bright gift of joy.**

A POWERFUL PROMISE

Gather kids and say: **We've been learning that joy doesn't stop here on earth but goes on forever in our heavenly home. We've discovered that**

the joy in heaven will be the brightest kind of joy and that Jesus will be at the center of this glorious joy. And we've reviewed our Mighty Memory Verse that says (lead kids in repeating Psalm 92:4 and the extra-challenge verse, if you've been learning it), **"For you make me glad by your deeds, O LORD; I sing for joy at the works of your hands."**

Have kids join hands. Say: **God has given us so much joy and promises even greater joy to come. Let's give God joy by thanking him for all he does for us.** Pray: **Dear Lord, we are amazed at the wondrous joy you offer us here and in our heavenly home. With all you do and all you plan for us, you tell us you love us. We love you too, and we want to thank you for the joy you give that helps us have hope, faith, and patience through hard times. We love you! Amen.**

Before kids leave, allow five or ten minutes to complete the Whiz Quiz from page 114. If you run out of time, be sure to do this page first thing next week. The Whiz Quiz is an invaluable tool that allows kids, teachers, and parents see what kids have learned in the previous three weeks.

Read aloud Revelation 12:12a, then end with this responsive good-bye:
Leader: **May the Lord's joy be with you.**
Children: **And also with you!**

Distribute the Power Page! take-home papers as kids are leaving. Thank children for coming and encourage them to let their Bright Joy-Lights shine as they thank the Lord for the joy he gives us today and promises us tomorrow.

POWER PAGE!

SCRAMBLED SCRIPTURE

Read Revelation 21:23 and unscramble the words in the Word Bank to complete the verse. Then you'll know the **JOY** we will have in our heavenly home!

"The _____ does not _____ the _____ or the _____ to _____ on it, for the _____ of _____ gives it _____, and the _____ is its _____."

WORD BANK

plam	nomo
githl	yict
neshi	oGd
deen	nus
goylr	baLm

JOY SHINES

Make this pretty centerpiece to enjoy as you remind your family about the shining joy that will be ours in our heavenly home.

Use *small nails* to poke holes in an *aluminum pie pan* (the disposable kind). Place a *tea-light candle* on a *glass plate* and

have a grown-up light the candle. Then carefully set the pan upside down on the plate. *The candle light will shine and glitter in joyous light!*

Crazy Circuit Board

Follow the arrows to plug in the missing letters from Psalm 92:4.

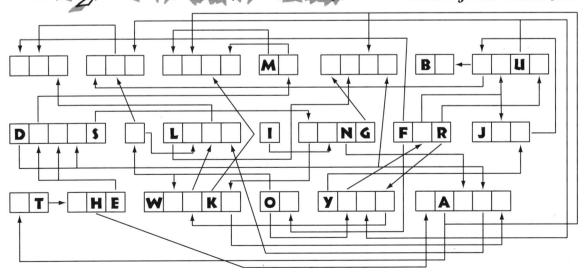

WHIZ QUIZ

Color in T (true) or F (false) to answer the following questions.

1. Our feelings change often. (T) (F)

2. Joy is constant, but feelings are temporary. (T) (F)

3. Joy isn't a choice. (T) (F)

4. Choosing joy gives us a positive attitude. (T) (F)

5. Joy will be brighter in heaven. (T) (F)

6. Nothing can take away our joy in Jesus. (T) (F)

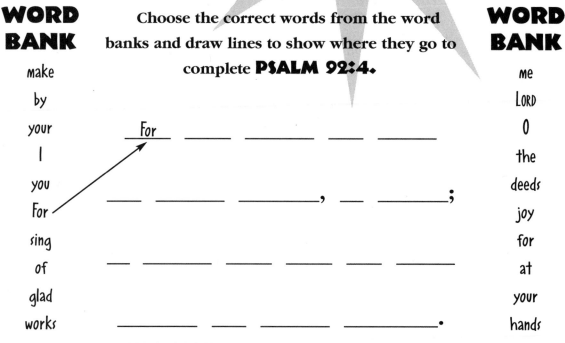

CHOOSE-N-USE

WORD BANK

make
by
your
I
you
For
sing
of
glad
works

Choose the correct words from the word banks and draw lines to show where they go to complete PSALM 92:4.

For ___ ___ ___ ___

___ ___ ___ ___, ___ ___;

___ ___ ___ ___ ___ ___

___ ___ ___ ___ ___.

WORD BANK

me
LORD
O
the
deeds
joy
for
at
your
hands

REVIEW LESSON

We will shout for joy when
you are victorious and will
lift up our banners in
the name of our God.
Psalm 20:5

JOY BUILDERS!

We build joy through knowing, loving, and following Jesus!

John 13:14, 15; 14:6
Romans 12:10
Hebrews 12:2

MIGHTY MEMORY VERSE

This is a review lesson of all four Mighty Memory Verses: Proverbs 16:20; 1 Peter 4:8; Psalm 119:41; Psalm 92:4.

SESSION OBJECTIVES

During this session, children will
★ understand that Jesus is the source of our joy
★ realize that Jesus and his joy are with us forever
★ learn what "infinite" means
★ discover that we have infinite joy and love through Christ

SESSION SUPPLIES

★ Bibles
★ T-shirts & sponges
★ squirty fabric paints (red, blue, purple, yellow)
★ newsprint & markers
★ glitter & fabric glue
★ cardboard boxes
★ scissors & pencils
★ carbon paper for tracing
★ photocopies of the Infinite Joy pattern (page 126)

BIBLE BACKGROUND

Think back to that ol' math class you took when you wondered if there would be any use in the lessons you learned. After all, who *really* needs to know or understand that there are numerical concepts that travel on forever into an infinite void of numbers? Well, without the concept of infinity, it might be hard to realize the never-ending nature of joy and the unbound love we have in Jesus! Consider an infinity sign: ∞. Cover up half of the left loop and the remaining shape is that of the Christian fish that reminds us of Jesus and his infinite nature. Jesus' love, salvation, forgiveness, and the joy we receive from accepting Jesus into our lives is infinite and able to carry us powerfully and lovingly through our very finite days in this world and into our eternal life in heaven!

How can kids really grasp what words such as *eternal, everlasting,* and *infinite* mean? After all, they've only been alive a few short years. But helping kids realize that the joy we have in Jesus goes on forever and follows us into our heavenly home is important. By linking the sign for infinity with the ichthus that reminds us of loving Jesus, kids will have a concrete symbol of forever that prompts them to remember the never-ending joy we have in Christ. Use this lively review lesson to recap the study of joy and to remind kids that the joy we have through Jesus goes on forever.

POWER FOCUS

Before class, you'll need to collect plastic bottles of squirty fabric paint that can be squeezed to make letters on fabric. You'll need red, yellow, blue, and purple paint (and additional colors, if you choose). Since this is the "grand finale" lesson of *Joy Builders,* the review project is extra fun and requires a bit more cost than average, "everyday" craft ideas. In addition to the squirty fabric paint, you'll need a white T-shirt for each child, sponges to sponge-paint with, pencils and carbon paper to transfer patterns to the shirts, and squares of cardboard to place inside the shirts so the wet paint doesn't "glue" the fronts and backs of the shirts together. For this activity, you'll need T-shirts, pencils, carbon paper, cardboard squares, and photocopies of the Infinite Joy pattern from page 126 for each child.

Welcome kids to class and have them sit in a circle. Say: **For the past several weeks, we've been discovering a lot of things about joy. We've learned where joy comes from, how joy helps us through hard times, how joy can be spread to others, and that joy from Jesus lasts a lifetime. We also discovered that Jesus had joy because of his love for us.** Read aloud Hebrews 12:2, then say: **Jesus even had joy as he endured the cross. His joy was for his heavenly Father and because Jesus knew he was giving his life so we could be forgiven and live close to God. Because of Jesus' great joy, we have joy. It is like Jesus' joy has been transferred to us.**

Today we'll end our study of joy by making awesome T-shirts that remind us of the joy we have when we know, love, and follow Jesus. We'll be making our wearable projects as we review all we've learned over the past few weeks. First, to remind us how Jesus transfers his joy to us, we need to transfer a pattern to your T-shirts.

Distribute the T-shirts, patterns, pencils, and cardboard squares. Have kids find a hard surface to work on, such as a table or a hard floor. Show kids how to slide the cardboard squares inside the T-shirts and smooth the fronts of the shirts over the cardboard. Place carbon on the T-shirts, shiny side down, and set the patterns on top of the carbon. (For younger kids, you may want to tape the pattern pages and carbon paper together and tape them both to the fronts of the shirts to avoid slippage.) Have kids trace over the pattern using their pencils, applying medium pressure but not enough to tear the patterns. The infinity design and words should transfer to the T-shirts and be ready to paint over with fabric paints as the lesson progresses.

When the patterns are in place, say: **Now let's discover what this funny looking symbol on your shirts stands for and how it relates to Jesus and his never-ending joy.**

POWER POINTERS

Photocopy all of the Mighty Memory Verses from page 127 on bright paper for kids to practice at home. Remember: reinforcement means memory!

THE MIGHTY MESSAGE

Before this activity, have the squirty bottles of fabric paint ready to go. You'll also need to draw the following review signs on sheets of newsprint: a sun (morning), a One Way sign (one way to God), a smile (happiness), a heart (joy or love), an ichthus (Jesus), a cross (Jesus' salvation, forgiveness), happy faces (people), an infinity sign (∞—forever, never ending). Place the signs in a pile in the center of the room.

Have kids form a large circle around the newsprint signs, then number off by fives. Say: **During our study of joy, we've had several signs and symbols to look at.** Hold up the signs and tell what each one signifies. Then continue: **Let's use those signs and symbols now as we review the important truths we've learned about joy and where it comes from. I'll read a verse or two, then call out a number from one to five. If your number is called, hop to the center of the room and choose the sign that best represents the verse. Then we'll answer a few questions before finding the next sign.**

Read aloud Matthew 22:33 and Mark 6:6b and call out a number. Have kids hop to the signs and hold up the *ichthus* or *cross* (Jesus—for his teaching) and the *people* (who Jesus taught). Have kids explain why these signs were chosen or any signs they might be holding, such as the heart for the loving way Jesus taught or the joy he imparted. Then ask:

★ **In what ways do Jesus' teachings bring us joy?**

★ **How does obeying Jesus' teaching make us happy?**

Read aloud John 13:14, 15 and Galatians 5:13b and call out a number. Have kids hold up the *ichthus* or *cross* (Jesus for serving others) and the *people* (disciples or us for Jesus modeling servanthood). Have kids explain their choices, then ask:

★ **Why did Jesus serve his disciples and teach us to serve too?**

★ **How can serving others bring us joy?**

Read aloud Romans 12:10 and call out a number. Have kids hop to the signs and hold up the *heart* (for loving others and the joy it brings) and the *people* (who we accept and love). Have kids explain their choices, then ask:

★ **How does accepting the unlovable bring joy to them? us? God?**

★ **Why should we try to love even our enemies?**

Read aloud Hebrews 12:2 and call out a number. Have kids hop to the signs and hold up the *ichthus* or *cross* (Jesus—for his salvation, forgiveness, and death on the cross), the *heart* (love from Jesus), or even the *smile* (gladness and thanksgiving we feel from being forgiven). Have kids explain their choices, then ask:

★ **How could Jesus have felt joy at the cross?**

★ **In what ways does Jesus' forgiveness and salvation bring us joy?**

Read aloud John 14:6 and Psalm 90:14 and call out a number. Have kids hold up the *One Way* sign (only one way to God), the *sun* (express joy through singing in the morning), and the *heart* (Jesus' unfailing love). Have kids explain their choices, then ask:

★ **What is our only way to find God and eternal life?**

★ **How does obeying and loving Jesus help us find God and joy?**

Read aloud Psalm 68:3 and 1 Thessalonians 5:16 and call out a number. Have kids hold up the *heart* (joy and rejoicing) and the *smile* (gladness, happiness). Have kids explain their choices, then ask:

★ **How does loving God and living as he desires strengthen our faith?**

★ **Why is it good to choose a joyful attitude throughout our lives?**

Say: **We've used all the signs but one—the infinity sign.** Hold the sign up, then say: **The symbol for infinity is like a sideways eight. It is a symbol used in mathematics to mean "never ending" or "forever." Why is this a good symbol to think of when we think of joy from Jesus?**

Allow kids to share their thoughts, then hold up the ichthus sign and say: **See how similar the ichthus, which stands for Jesus, and the infinity** sign are? In fact, if we cover up this portion of the infinity sign (cover the lower left portion of the sign so it makes an ichthus fish), **it makes an ichthus! That's neat, because it reminds us about the eternal, never-ending nature of Jesus, his love, and the joy we have in Christ! You can say that we have "infinite joy!"** Now cover the ichthus section to reveal the letter C at the end of the infinity sign. **And here's the C that stands for Christ, who brings us infinite joy!**

Let's use fabric paints to sponge-paint a two-color infinity sign on your T-shirts. Use one color for the ichthus portion and another color for the C. Help kids use small sponges to daub over the outlines of the infinity sign, using two colors. Be sure the letter C is facing the right direction! Then set the shirts aside to dry.

Say: **Review times are fun because they give us a chance to see all we've learned and to lock that learning in place. Let's get any wiggles out by joyously reviewing the Joy Rap we learned a few weeks ago!** Keep the paints and sponges handy.

THE MESSAGE IN MOTION

Be sure the T-shirts aren't in the way of kids moving around the room during the lively Joy Rap. Then lead kids in repeating the words to the Joy Rap from page 95 and making up their own motions to accompany the words. Add in the following verse, then end by rapping the chorus once more.

> *Just think of all we have through Jesus—*
> *Infinite joy that forgives and frees us!*
> *Never-ending gladness from Jesus' grace—*
> *And joy in our HEARTS that stays in place!*

After rapping, have kids give each other high fives, then sit in place. Say: **Remember when we discovered that feelings such as sadness, anger, frustration, and even being everyday happy are temporary and depend on our situations? Those feelings just live on our faces and can change in a flash! But the joy we have through Jesus is never-ending joy and lives forever in our hearts.**

Invite two volunteers to read aloud 2 Corinthians 4:17, 18. Say: **These verses remind us that most things are temporary or momentary and only last for a short time. But joy from Jesus and his love and salvation are never ending. In other words, they are infinite! The word *infinite* comes from the word *infinity*—like our infinity signs—and means eternal or never ending, just as our joy in Jesus is. Let's sponge-paint and squeeze-paint the words "Infinite Joy" on our T-shirts to remind us that Jesus' love brings us joy that can never be taken away and never ends.**

Have kids first paint the word "Infinite" by squeezing fabric paint over the letters on their shirts. Caution kids to be very careful not to smudge or smear the paint and to be sure and paint left to right across the word. Then have kids use small sponges to sponge-paint the word "Joy" on their shirts, again being careful not to smudge the paint.

When the words are painted, sprinkle a bit of glitter on the word "Joy." The wet paint will allow the glitter to stick, but don't press the glitter into the painted letters, since they may smear.

Set the shirts aside to begin drying. Say: **Your Infinite Joy T-shirts look awesome! They'll be so cool to wear, and you can explain the ichthus-infinity sign to others as you remind them about the infinite, never-ending joy we have through Jesus! You've been reviewing everything so well today. Let's see how well you remember the Mighty Memory Verses we've learned over the last several weeks.**

SUPER SCRIPTURE

Before class, make three photocopies of the Scripture Strips from page 127. (If you have more than twelve kids in class, prepare another copy or two of the verses.) Cut the Mighty Memory Verses apart (and the extra-challenge verses, if you've been learning them), then cut each verse into three sections. Be sure you have the rebus verses from Revelation that kids made last week. You'll be reading those verses today.

Have kids sit in a circle and hand each child a puzzle piece. Then place the rest of the pieces in the center of the circle. Begin by having one child read his portion of a verse. If anyone has a portion that goes with the verse to help complete it, she must place her piece with the asker's puzzle piece, then draw another piece from the pile. Continue in this manner until all the verses have been assembled. Read each Mighty Memory Verse aloud, then go around the circle and let kids repeat their favorite Mighty Memory Verses from the ones learned. Then ask:

★ **In what ways does it help us to learn God's Word?**

★ **How does learning and using God's Word bring us joy? bring joy to God?**

Say: **God's Word holds the keys to life, getting along with others, obeying God, and finding joy that lasts a lifetime and beyond. And this joy is like a bright light that shines inside our hearts. Remember our rebus verses from last week that helped us discover the pure, bright joy we'll find in our heavenly home?**

Have kids read the rebus verses from last week with you. Then say: **Let's add bright lights and sparkles to our T-shirts to remind us of the bright, unblocked joy we'll find in our heavenly home one day.**

Use fabric glue and glitter to make bright stars and swirls on the T-shirts, but avoiding the wet-paint areas. Then set the shirts aside to dry. The shirts will be dry by next meeting time and can be worn and washed safely. If you're brave, let kids' parents carry their shirts home, being very careful not to smear wet glue or paint. Clothes hangers might work well to tote the shirts home more safely.

A POWERFUL PROMISE

Gather kids in a circle and say: **What a great time we've had reviewing all we've discovered about joy. We know that true joy comes from Jesus and lasts for an infinite time. We know that feelings we have day to day are temporary but that joy is never ending. We've discovered that knowing, loving, and following Jesus are keys to locking joy in our hearts. And we've learned that there are many ways to express joy. Let's close our joyous time together by expressing our joy for Jesus through the Joy Song!**

Lead kids in singing the Joy Song (page 17). Then read aloud Proverbs 23:18 and 1 Thessalonians 5:16, then end with this responsive good-bye:

Leader: **May the joy of Jesus always be with you.**

Children: **And also with you!**

Thank children for coming and encourage them to thank Jesus for his infinite joy every day this week and forever!

BEE-ATTITUDES

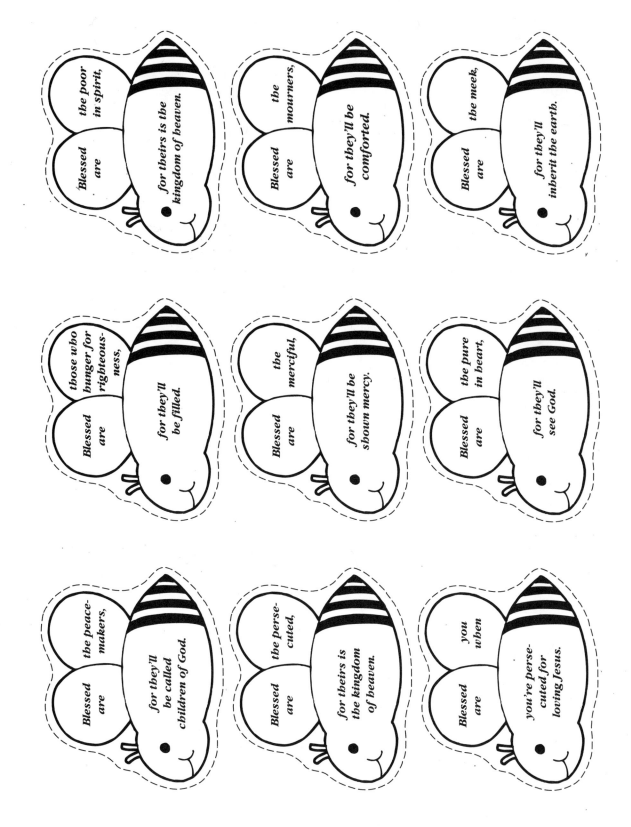

Blessed are the poor in spirit, for theirs is the kingdom of heaven.

Blessed are the mourners, for they'll be comforted.

Blessed are the meek, for they'll inherit the earth.

Blessed are those who hunger for righteousness, for they'll be filled.

Blessed are the merciful, for they'll be shown mercy.

Blessed are the pure in heart, for they'll see God.

Blessed are the peacemakers, for they'll be called children of God.

Blessed are the persecuted, for theirs is the kingdom of heaven.

Blessed are you when you're persecuted for loving Jesus.

CONSTANT OR CHANGING?

REBUS PICTURES

INFINITE JOY PATTERN

SCRIPTURE STRIPS

Whoever gives heed to instruction prospers, and blessed is he who trusts in the LORD. *Proverbs 16:20*

For no one can lay any foundation other than the one already laid, which is Jesus Christ. *1 Corinthians 3:11*

Above all, love each other deeply, because love covers over a multitude of sins. *1 Peter 4:8*

And over all these virtues put on love, which binds them all together in perfect unity. *Colossians 3:14*

May your unfailing love come to me, O LORD, your salvation according to your promise. *Psalm 119:41*

I am the way and the truth and the life. No one comes to the Father except through me. *John 14:6*

For you make me glad by your deeds, O LORD; I sing for joy at the works of your hands. *Psalm 92:4*

The LORD is my strength and my shield; my heart trusts in him, and I am helped. *Psalm 28:7a*

POWER UP YOUR KIDS!

Now there are eight Power Builders books to empower your kids for a lifetime of faith! Susan Lingo's Power Builders curriculum engages kids in learning as much as in fun! Each topical 13-lesson book includes Bible-bound, Scripture-sound, kid-pleasing, life-changing lessons—PLUS teacher training and ways to tell if your kids are really learning. What a powerful combination!

  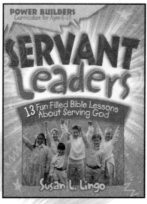 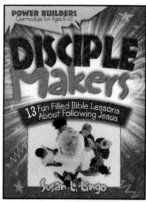

Value Seekers
(42111)
Help kids transform their lives by seeking, recognizing, and living by the values Jesus taught.

Faith Finders
(42112)
Direct kids to discover their own faith in God through Jesus and the Holy Spirit.

Servant Leaders
(42113)
Motivate kids to develop a life-long attitude of serving God and others by examining the lives of Bible times servants.

Disciple Makers
(42114)
Lead kids to know more about Jesus and equip them to follow Jesus and to disciple others.

 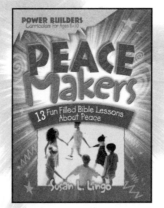 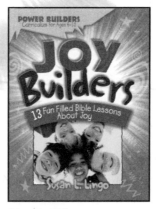 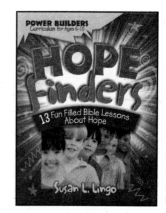

Power Boosters
(42115)
Empower your kids by helping them discover God's power to change their lives.

Peace Makers
(42116)
Build your kids' abilities to be at peace with God, others, and themselves.

Joy Builders
(42117)
Encourage kids to discover the joy of the Lord and to build on that joy by getting to know Jesus more and more.

Hope Finders
(42118)
Share the hope kids can find in knowing and obeying God and help them live with an eternal hope.

Look for these and other excellent Christian education products by Standard Publishing at your local Christian bookstore or order directly from Standard Publishing by calling 1-800-482-2060.